Your **Roadmap** to
Project Management Results
USING FIVE SIMPLE CHECKLISTS

Stephen Hightower

First printing, 2019 – Printed in the United States of America.

ISBN: 9781706213994

Your **Roadmap** to
Project Management Results
USING FIVE SIMPLE CHECKLISTS

Acknowledgements

Writing a book for the first time is a journey that takes many twists and turns. I thought about the concept several years ago, started writing the manuscript in 2013, and then changed the approach entirely half-way through it. It seems I was constantly revising or overthinking my material. I decided to set a goal to complete the book in 2019 and finally it's published. Setting your mind on accomplishing important goals in your life and then following through on those promises is a constant challenge and I've been doing better with that, but still have miles to go. Project management is very similar, a winding road of ups and downs with curves and detours, but if you stay focused on the basics and keep pushing forward you'll finish.

Project management is a critical skill that you need because in all aspects your life and career, you're managing projects. Like most people, you're in the continual pursuit of improving and getting better each day. Sometimes you lose your focus and get distracted with other priorities, but if you keep focused on the important things, you'll end up in the right place.

I want to thank my wife, Jacquelyn, who is a source of inspiration, especially on endurance and mental toughness. She is a survivor of Acute Lymphoblastic Leukemia, with discouraging odds for success, she received a Bone Marrow Transplant from an unrelated donor out of Norway. 19 years later, and with many set-backs along the way, she is doing great.

Her outlook and mindset are amazing, especially for all she's had to endure. She inspires me every day, through her humor and wit that makes me laugh and not take myself too seriously. As she's fond of saying when I get too serious, "You're not the boss of me".

I'd like to thank my partners at Flow Consulting who have taught me so much about a career in consulting and doing it well.

I want to thank my dear friends, Tom Ward and Richard Wright for reviewing, editing and providing the feedback that allowed me to finish this book. Friends who give back to you are the "true gifts" in your life.

Lastly, I want to thank my daughter Madelyn, who introduced me to yoga and frequently reminds me I'm not always the smartest person in the room.

I hope you enjoy the book and use the *Five Simple Checklists* to achieve tremendous results.

Table of Contents

Foreword

I've managed projects most of my professional life that range from intense, six-week sprints to multi-year, multi-million-dollar efforts. Project management wasn't something I planned on doing when I started my career, but looking back, it was a tremendous opportunity which helped shape my career and prepared me for what I'm doing today. I wrote this book to provide a template for new project managers to utilize as a roadmap for their projects and for experienced project managers who might not be getting optimal results.

I managed my first large multi-million-dollar project many years ago. I was unsure how to approach it and luckily, I had a very seasoned senior project manager who guided and instructed me to do things correctly. This was in an era where you were often told what to do without any input. This project was a huge, very visible initiative that consolidated the duplicate IT infrastructure (data centers, help desks, procurement, telecommunications) across the company.

It was necessary due to a recent merger that was looking for a large cost reduction commitment of $140,000,000 over a five-year period.

I was somewhat apprehensive about the assignment, but very excited to be able to have such a significant impact on the merger of two major corporations. This project spanned multiple locations and had multiple team members that already had full time jobs. I knew very little about the discipline of project management, and I didn't have the background to take on the task. As it turned out, I had a lot of experienced resources around me that would provide support and guidance. Not every organization has experienced project managers and finding a mentor as a novice project manager is invaluable.

Project management is a critical skill that is required to succeed in most organizations. If you are able to manage complexity, have a high tolerance for ambiguity and are disciplined in your approach, most things are easy. Not all of us have those skill sets, so what do you do? Where do you start?

The discipline of project management is found in the *Project Management Body of Knowledge (PMBOK)*. The latest publication, the 6th edition, was published in September of 2017. The *PMBOK* is extensive in its coverage of the project management discipline and covers areas such as:

- Foundational standards
- Practice Standards and Frameworks
- Practice Guides
- Lexicon of Project Management Terms

The 6th edition is about 8.2 inches wide, 1.1 inches thick, and 11.8 inches long. It weighs about 3.4 pounds and has 756 pages divided in 19 chapters and 6 appendices.

As a new project manager, diving into a book that massive can be overwhelming to say the least. Another option is to take advantage of the lessons I have learned through years of experience and leverage the approach I've outlined in this book to help solve problems and manage your projects successfully. This book is not a replacement for the *PMBOK*, or the knowledge contained in it. Rather, this book is a framework that I developed over a period of many years that can be used to reduce risk and increase the quality of the projects you are managing.

This book will provide you with *Five Simple Checklists* for the lifecycle of project management and how to apply tools from the Lean discipline. Lean is the systematic method for elimination of waste within your production system. Lean has typically been applied in a manufacturing environment but is just as applicable in a services environment and for knowledge workers. The principles are focused on reducing waste and improving efficiencies throughout your processes. The philosophy is derived from the *Toyota Production System (TPS)*. The book, *The Machine that Changed the World*, was written in 1991 and was based on the Massachusetts Institute of Technology's $5 Million, 5 year study on the future of the automobile. It was authored by James P. Womack, Daniel T. Jones, and Daniel Roos.

I've witnessed project management applied in large and small companies, across many industries and it parallels the stories told in, *The Machine that Changed the World*. Project managers typically operate much like the artisan craftsmen who made automobiles before Henry Ford revolutionized automobile mass production. They each had their own approach which they successfully used throughout their career, but they didn't have an approach for delivering standard work each time that would lead to a consistent level of quality.

There are many questions you have when you're given a project to manage, especially for the first time.

- How do I know I'm on schedule?
- How will I be able to hit my cost targets?
- How do I make sure everyone is on the same page and understands what we're doing?
- How do I address if I'm behind schedule or overrunning cost targets on my project?

I've seen project management run the gamut from an ad-hoc approach to a highly disciplined and repeatable process with common processes. If you or your organization have trouble managing projects, then this book can help you achieve a higher level of consistent, repeatable processes and quality while reducing your risk. Follow this roadmap and it will make you a *"Problem Solver"* and a sought after resource to manage even bigger projects.

CHAPTER 1

Project Management

[The Lifecycle of a Project]

"Life is like riding a bicycle, to keep your balance, you must keep riding"

-Albert Einstein

A project is a temporary endeavor undertaken to create a unique product, service or result. Project management is the process of managing several related goals focused on implementing new capabilities or services for an organization.

Did you know that over 70% of all technology projects are considered failures[1]. Is your project doomed from the start? How do you manage complexity and deliver projects on time and within

---

1   Standish Report

budget? How do you know you're taking the right steps to manage your project for success?

The *Project Management Body of Knowledge (PMBOK)* is a set of standard terminology and guidelines (the body of knowledge) for project management. It provides a common language for project managers. Much of the *PMBOK* is unique to project management e.g. *Earned Value Management (EVM)* and *Work Breakdown Structure (WBS)*. It overlaps with general management; including planning, organizing, staffing, executing, and controlling the operations of the organization. The first *PMBOK* guide was published in 1996 and the 6th edition was published September 6th, 2017.

The *Project Management Body of Knowledge (PMBOK),* is generally recognized as a good practice of project management. "Generally recognized" means the methods and practices described are applicable to most projects most of the time and there is a consensus about their value and usefulness. "Good practice" means there is a general agreement that when applying the knowledge, skills, tools, and techniques there is an enhanced chance of success over many projects. Do you need to be knowledgeable in all the material in the *PMBOK*?

In my opinion, the *PMBOK* has become a document that is very complex. Most people are a little intimidated when they think about having to read, understand and retain 978 pages of knowledge. How do you simplify this content to something that is useful for the average person trying to manage a project? I prefer to have a condensed version that doesn't drag things out and gets to the point. Project management is like most things in life, if you understand the basics and apply them consistently, you'll cover the majority of the issues you'll encounter.

This book will provide project managers with an approach to simplify the complexity that has been compiled in the *Project Management Body of Knowledge (PMBOK)*. Managing projects is akin to managing chaos in many companies. I've seen so many different approaches that are applied with varying results.

Most companies will assign a project to an individual who already has a full-time job. The resources assigned to the team are typically fully employed as well. This is the greatest risk in most companies no matter if they are $1M in annual revenue or $100B in annual revenue. Everyone is busy, and they don't have a disciplined approach to complete projects successfully. In many cases, they are told by the boss "just make it happen and don't bother me with the details."

The tools and checklists provided in this book will give you a roadmap to follow and will simplify your approach to managing projects and reducing your risk. You wouldn't drive from San Diego, California to Orlando, Florida without having a plan or using tools to help map the route to take, would you? It seems you would want to plan your trip, understand the distance, the estimated duration and plan any stops if you needed to rest or to spend the night.

Follow the tools and checklists to give you a consistent approach that will be repeatable throughout the project lifecycle and apply the principles of Lean to reduce the waste that is present when you manage projects. The *Five Simple Checklists* are straightforward. You will learn to use several metrics that will provide you with quantitative insight as to whether you are meeting your cost and schedule targets.

IF YOU CAN'T SEE IT, THEN YOU CAN'T MEASURE IT
IF YOU CAN'T MEASURE IT, THEN YOU CAN'T MANAGE IT
IF YOU CAN'T MANAGE IT, THEN YOU CAN'T IMPROVE IT

Project management is about accountability and execution. When you're running a company or an organization and select someone to lead an important project, you expect full accountability for the effort. You don't want excuses or your project manager to make the comment, "I was just going to take care of that", after you pointed out the issue. I'm always perplexed when I work with project managers that don't exhibit accountability and are constantly missing their targets. They provide excuses rather than answers and mitigation plans. Guess what, every project has issues and you need to be the problem solver because companies value and reward problem solvers.

I've developed the *Five Simple Checklists* to give project managers an approach that's simple and straight forward to use. You will have a roadmap that you can follow with these Checklists to manage your projects for success. You don't have to spend a tremendous amount of time to understand the concepts and you can simplify the complexity that often exists in project management. Complexity in any endeavor will cloud the issues and take your focus away from the critical tasks you must accomplish to be successful.

The *Five Simple Checklists* in this book will provide you with a roadmap for project management that will arm you with an approach to manage projects that will meet your schedule and cost targets. The key to this approach is to manage with data and to have accountability across your project team. To successfully manage your projects will require you to be data driven. Reliance on your "gut instinct" or feel for the project is not the way to go. While you don't have to employ three decimal point accuracy for the project metrics which will be fluid and subject to constant adjustments, you will, however, need to use proper estimating techniques.

The *Five Simple Checklists* are your roadmap to quantify the areas that matter and, if followed, will improve your performance. In addition, it will allow you to be more proactive. You will be able to address issues sooner and provide pro-active risk mitigation for your critical issues. The more you use the *Five Simple Checklists* and educate your team on the process, the more successful you will become managing projects.

Managing projects should be a core competency for anyone who wants to advance in their career and take on increasing responsibilities. The *PMBOK* is quite extensive and there are several certifications that individuals can be tested on to prove area competence. The *PMBOK* has five process groups that are used as the quality framework for managing the lifecycle of any project. The Project Management Lifecycle is a framework that's defined by the following five processes:

INITIATING PROCESS

- Projects are assigned to qualified project managers who are trained in the discipline. **Checklists (PSS and APM).**
- Project Kickoff - Announcement and kickoff with key stakeholders. Scope and schedule are clearly defined. The project manager will set up a log for the project, and an action item repository. **Checklists (PSS, CFS or APM).**

PLANNING PROCESS

- The project will be setup in your project management tool based on the estimate usually defined by a *Work Breakdown Structure (WBS)* in the proposal. Named resources are allocated to the plan. **Checklists (PSS or APM).**

EXECUTING PROCESS

- Adjust schedule and hours for resources. The *Estimate to Complete (ETC)* and *Estimate at Completion (EAC)* are used to manage cost. Request change orders or add services as needed. Impact sheet is completed by the project manager for scope changes. **Checklists (APM, MYS, CFS).**

MONITORING AND CONTROLLING PROCESS

- Project Management Reviews - Monthly reviews are scheduled with the principle to review key metrics *(Schedule Performance Index(SPI), ETC, EAC)* on projects. Identify scope changes, issues with customer or project. **Checklists (MYS, CFS).**
- Action Item Tracking - Each review will document the discussion and the actions taken. Project planning will track and monitor action item progress. Weekly updates will be provided on actions. **Checklists (CFS).**

CLOSING PROCESS

- Your project is finished, and you need to close it with the proper artifacts for continuous learning. **Checklists (CPS).**

PROCESSES ARE DESCRIBED IN TERMS OF:

- Inputs (documents, plans, designs, etc.)
- Tools and Techniques (mechanisms applied to inputs)
- Outputs (documents, plans, designs, etc.)

The Project Management Lifecycle is represented by the following diagram:

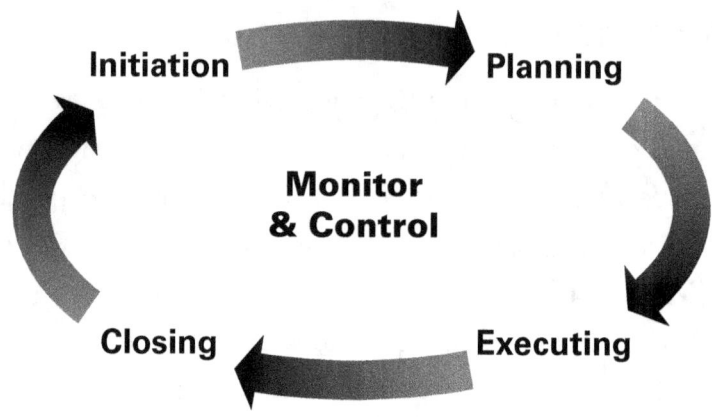

The *PMBOK* has five process groups and ten knowledge areas. The process groups are the quality framework that define the Project Management Lifecycle. Using this approach provides the quality needed to manage projects successfully. The knowledge areas are as follows:

- Integration
- Scope
- Time
- Cost
- Quality
- Procurement
- Human Resources
- Communications
- Risk Management
- Stakeholder Management

The *Five Simple Checklists* are used to support the lifecycle and provide you with a clear and simple roadmap that will improve the quality of the services you are providing for managing projects. For new project managers, this approach will maximize your chances for success, even if you don't have 20 years of experience.

All projects have a beginning and an end, sometimes a bad ending but none the less, they all end. The critical part is the definition and scoping of the project. The first two phases are critical to getting off to the right start with your project (Initiating and Planning). "How it begins, is how it ends", so you need to build momentum and repeatability at the start. The next three phases (Executing, Monitoring & Controlling and Closing) are about delivering results.

In each phase you will have different artifacts/deliverables you will use to make sure that you're hitting all the elements in the checklist. This starts with a well-documented problem statement and ends with the celebration for completing your project. The checklists are mapped to the project lifecycle and the artifacts support your service delivery.

The following diagram shows you how the *Five Simple Checklists* are used across the Project Management Lifecycle.

Five Simple Checklists				
PSS (Project Startup Standards)	**APM** (Agile Project Management)	**CFS** (Communicate for Success)	**MYS** (Manage Your Schedule)	**CPS** (Closing Projects Successfully)
Project Management Lifecycle				
Initiating	Initiating	Initiating	Executing	Closing
Planning	Planning	Planning	Monitoring & Controlling	
	Executing	Executing		
	Monitoring & Controlling	Monitoring & Controlling		
Checklist Artifacts				
Problem Statement	User Stories	Sponsor Communication	Updated Schedule	Original Scope
Scope/Charter	Kanban Board	Weekly Key Messages	Percent Complete	Final Scope
Day in the Life (DITL)	Day in the Life (DITL)	Weekly Project Status	Cost Performance Index (CPI)	Lessons Learned
Business Case	Sprints	Scope Change Log	Performance Index (SPI)	Financial Shutdown
RACI	Test Cases	Risk Register	Resource Schedule	Maintenance Plans
Schedule	Communication	Schedule Impacts	Risk Register	Stakeholder Communication
Risk Register		Resource Changes		Celebration

The ***PSS Checklist (Project Startup Standards)*** is your first step to initiating the project with the critical elements to be successful. *Initiating* is defining the scope of the effort and developing a case for change. The case for change can be a business case with a positive Return on Investment (ROI), or a risk to be mitigated for compliance efforts like Sarbanes Oxley (SOX), Health Insurance Portability and Accountability Act (HIPAA), the General Data Protection Regulation (GDPR), or adding new capabilities to meet competitive threats in the marketplace. You need to develop a project charter that guides your project for definition, scope and stakeholders. The charter is sometimes referred to as a project initiation document. If you're managing a software project, you'll want to use the *Agile Project Management (APM) Checklist* and follow it to make sure you're planning and executing appropriately. I've added a key step in the *PSS Checklist* that goes beyond the traditional view on project management. The step is the *Day in the Life (DITL)* that provides a clear picture of what happens when you complete the project. Chapter 2 will go into more detail with examples for you.

The **APM Checklist (Agile Project Management)** is used to develop your user stories, to prioritize and map your stories to your software development sprints. I manage software development vendors for many of my clients and use the *APM Checklist* to ensure we get a quality product that meets our requirements. You would think if your vendor follows the Agile methodology that you would be able to follow their approach, but in my experience it's not always transparent. You are paying for the work being performed, so you should be able to follow the vendor's approach. The *APM Checklist* has a specific section for execution that follows the daily activities. It's essential to spend the time to develop the plans for how you will execute on your project. The time you spend planning will be correlated to having a properly scoped project. Remember, "measure twice and cut once". Plan and prepare in a careful, thoughtful manner before taking action. This is one of the hardest things to do when managing a project, especially if there is an urgent and pressing problem. Resisting the pressure to act quickly versus thoroughly will ensure a more favorable outcome.

The **CFS Checklist (Communicate for Success)** is used to identify the different channels for communication, the artifacts used and the frequency of the communication. Managing the communication is so critical because people get busy and they stop paying attention unless you are laser focused on execution. With all the distractions and interruptions that occur in the workplace today, you really need to follow your checklists to meet your commitments. Don't assume because you sent an email that people will read it or understand it.

The **MYS Checklist (Manage your Schedule)** is used to keep your critical metrics updated in order to track the progress being made against the cost and schedule. You'll look at your resource plans, the risk register and check the scope of work to make sure you're executing the in-scope activities. Out of scope will occur, and you will need to manage these changes at the time they happen. Don't wait to document the change because you'll either forget about it or you'll have another urgent priority that will prevent you from taking action.

The **CPS Checklist (Closing Projects Successfully)** is used to document the results and drive continuous improvement across your organization. Using the *CPS Checklist* isn't a significant effort, but it's important to recognize individuals and celebrate as a team all the amazing things you've accomplished during that hectic time. It's a great way to make sure you've closed with your customer on the results of the project. It's a good way to drive best practices on your projects based on "lessons learned" and customer feedback. These efforts drive continued customer satisfaction and the opportunity for you to take on the next challenge that will come your way as you "slay the dragons".

In project management, there is the concept known as the *Triple Constraint*. The *Triple Constrainttt* is defined by quality (scope), cost (resources) and schedule (time). Understanding this concept is a basic requirement for any project manager. If project management were a stool, each of these elements would be an equally, necessary leg.

These three elements of a project are essential and must work in harmony with each other. When one of these elements is restricted or extended, the other two elements will also need to be either restricted or reduced in some way or extended or increased to offset the changes. Using the *Five Simple Checklists* approach will provide you with the steps needed to manage the *Triple Constraint*.

Communication covers many aspects of the project and the lifecycle of project management. I once worked on a project where we were behind schedule, over cost and under so much pressure, I was sure everyone would be fired. Instead, we had a project manager that was an overachiever in communication and made sure to over communicate to all the stakeholders on a regular and frequent basis.

As a result, no one ever had to wonder or ask about status because he made sure everyone had the most current information. Rather than being punished for the project being behind schedule and over cost he was given an award for how well he communicated and eventually completed the project successfully. This goes against many project managers' instincts when they find themselves in this situation, which is why it's so important to have this outlined from the beginning.

WITH THE *TRIPLE CONSTRAINT*, YOU CAN CHANGE TWO ELEMENTS BUT NOT ALL THREE:

What is a project? It's a temporary endeavor undertaken to create a unique product, service or result. A project is temporary in that it has a defined beginning and ending time, with a defined scope and resources.

A project is unique, in that it IS NOT a routine operation. It does have a specific set of operations designed to accomplish a singular goal. A project team often includes people who don't usually work together. Sometimes they are from different organizations and work across multiple geographies.

Examples of projects are the development of software for an improved business process, the construction of a building or bridge, the relief effort after a natural disaster, or the expansion of sales into a new geographic market. All projects must be expertly managed to deliver the learning and integration, on-time, on-budget results that organizations need.

There are many tools, that can be used to manage projects. Tools like Microsoft Project, Monday.com, Smartsheet, etc., can all provide a collaborative work environment for geographically dispersed team members. There are a variety of tools that are available, but you should look for the following characteristics:

Cloud based
Collaborative
Ease of Use
Robust reporting and alerts
Dashboard capability

These tools allow everyone to see the tasks and interact together to achieve the objectives of the project. Developing the methodology for managing your project is more than just the project management tool that you use or the collaboration space that is created for your team. It's having a cohesive team that works together to meet the objectives of the project and share the belief each member makes a difference. Using the *Five Simple Checklists* approach will help you develop the right plan for your team.

I've learned that your project should not have so much detail that it requires a daily update. The more complex your project, the more details there will be, but you must strike the right balance.

Too many organizations don't apply a structured discipline or science to the management of projects. They leave "things" to chance in many cases which results in waste and additional expense. You want to apply a process to projects that you manage, and you want to do it in the most cost-effective way possible.

The primary questions project managers should answer are:

Is the project on schedule?
Is the project on budget?
Am I managing risks appropriately?
Do I communicate effectively?

To do this successfully, the project manager should understand and apply *Earned Value Management (EVM)* to their projects. *EVM* helps you answer the most critical questions (budget/schedule) with discipline and quantitative measurements. We're going to work through examples in the following chapters which you can use as you improve your project management skills with the *Five Simple Checklists* approach.

When most people hear that you want to use *EVM* as a model they freak out and think it's a lot of work, but in reality, it's not. It can actually save you work. It's not something where you'll always need three decimal point accuracy, but when you use it as a forecast it provides you a measure on your progress. I know some people will disagree with this approach, but in my experience, it works well when you apply it correctly.

The majority of my career was spent working for Lockheed Martin. I retired from Lockheed Martin in 2011 as the Chief Information Officer of the Global Training and Logistics business unit and started consulting with a focus on Private Equity portfolio companies. During my career at Lockheed Martin, we had excellent training across the project management discipline and using Lean Six Sigma (LSS). We had a strong discipline around process and project management to be able to deliver complex projects across the company and to our customers. We had standards, Key Performance Indicators (KPI's) and were extremely well versed in the *PMBOK*. Project management was a primary competency for the company and project managers received extensive training. Even with all these tools there were still failures.

I have managed projects for individual business units and across the enterprise. These projects spanned from $50,000 to multi-million-dollar efforts that spanned multiple years. The majority of the projects were focused on technology implementations for business transformation, process improvements and consolidations that generated cost reductions.

In addition, there were facility consolidations, new construction projects, information security transformations and a number of other projects that influenced the development of the *Five Simple Checklists*. Most of the projects started with a problem statement that would lead to a business case, then a technology or product evaluation, and finally, approval to move forward. There were many stakeholders that weighed in on the reviews and the normal bureaucratic behaviors and politics that exist in a large organization. The best way to navigate through the process was to have data that drove your decisions and was used to manage your project. Data will take most of the emotion out of your projects. Generally, data does not lie.

Working for a large company, I had access to resources and standards that you would not see in smaller companies, particularly in Private Equity portfolio companies. We had processes, procedures, project structure and Key Process Indicators (KPI's) that were used extensively. The purpose of all the effort put into project management was to deliver to the customer, on schedule, on budget and with a high level of quality. In this world, you get the best and worst of large organizations. The best part is you have access to the resources, standards and processes as well as some very talented people. The worst is you have the downside of large organizations that have dysfunctional behaviors and a host of other issues that add to the complexity.

For example, we had a Systems Engineering set of standards that would be applied to projects whether they were $20M in scope or $50K. You have a different set of variables in both cases and the costs to apply that same framework to the $50K project whether it's needed or not will drive your costs to the point where you can't provide an affordable solution. We had no flexibility to adjust based on the problem, so when your only tool is a hammer, everything is a nail.

In many ways this is the same dilemma that drove software development to adopt Agile processes versus the traditional waterfall development methodology. You should adjust based on the complexity of your project, with what actually makes sense and minimizes the risk to deliver to your client. Common sense doesn't always work when people are fixated on using a methodology without using a reality-based approach.

After I began consulting for Private Equity I realized very quickly that the companies I was consulting for didn't have the resources and the knowledge in most cases to manage projects for success. Typically, they would assign a person who may or may not be the best fit to manage a project or they would hire me, which was clearly a better answer.

If they didn't hire me and assigned an individual, that person would do their best to be successful given their other demands, but rarely was able to perform to the company's expectation. The individuals would typically start taking action without any plan or baseline because they were under pressure to get something done. Project management has a set of disciplines that should be followed throughout the lifecycle of the project. I've put together the *Five Simple Checklists* that will mitigate your risks and help you become a more successful project manager without having to understand everything in the *PMBOK*.

Activity Without a Plan (AWP) is something I'll spend time on later in the book, but it's one of the most common issues that will lead to failure. People are typically unclear on the overall project because they don't have a charter or a scope of work that's precise, detailed and documented. They get direction verbally and manage based on the "crisis du jour".

In over thirty years of managing projects, I've had my share of success and failures. Through this experience, I've developed a set of criteria that when applied will mitigate your risks to ensure you have a successful outcome.

Managing projects effectively is one of the most important tasks in any organization. Doing it well brings greater responsibilities and not managing projects well is a recipe for disaster. There is a clear discipline in project management that must be followed, but there are some unique challenges which will be critical to your success when you mange projects with shared resources. Learn how to put the right tools in place which will support the successful management of your projects.

I had a boss many years ago and one of his favorite sayings was, "complexity breeds cost". He would lecture his team over and over on this topic until we started to use the same language. He understood the "siren call" that technology has on engineers and their need to do something that's not been done before. He was focused on the delivery of the project and meeting the cost targets. If you don't address the basics and do them well, then you can't perform the advanced work that will generate more significant benefits. You will hear the term, "low hanging fruit" that we can gather doing the simple things, but there is another phrase in Six Sigma that says, "the sweetest fruit is at the top of the tree".

Execute on the basics and then climb the tree to get the sweetest fruit!

The approach outlined in this book will focus on eliminating waste in your processes. The reason this is important is because as a project manager you are a knowledge worker and knowledge workers tend to under estimate the amount of waste in their processes. Knowledge workers also tend to under estimate their time to complete a task consistently. Why is that? For example, you believe you have a task that will take you one hour to complete tomorrow morning for your boss. You are assuming that you have everything you need to complete the task and you will be able to pick up where you left off the last time you worked on the task.

As you start your task, you find you need to locate the reference materials you will use for the analysis. You review your materials and realize you have multiple copies of the document and have to spend time making sure you have the correct version. You review the version and orient yourself to the task to complete your analysis. The analysis requires you to obtain some additional information from a coworker, so you email them to get the data. The coworker is busy and doesn't respond to your email for a couple of hours, so you wait and move on to your next task. You receive three phone calls and five texts you have to respond to and every time you restart, you have to re-orient yourself on what you were doing before you were interrupted.

Finally, when your coworker sends you the information, it's the wrong version and you go back and forth with a couple more emails until finally you have what you need. While completing your analysis, you realize you should have had a meeting with your key stakeholders to get their inputs, but you're out of time and have to go with the information as it exists. Your boss is now frustrated and pressing you to complete the task and forward the analysis to him for review. Your time spent on the actual analysis may have been an hour, but with the waste in your process the total time spent was 4 hours. You assumed you had everything you needed and would be totally productive while working on it. Your assumption was incorrect.

THE 8 FORMS OF WASTE (TIMWOOD-I) FOR KNOWLEDGE WORKERS ARE:

1. **Unnecessary Transportation** - is using email ineffectively. An example of transportation waste is continuing to email back and forth with a coworker to ask questions that could easily have been resolved with a single phone call versus wasting time using email ineffectively.

2. **Too much Inventory** - You have too many versions of a spreadsheet that is being used for an analysis on a project. It becomes difficult to determine which is the most current version to use and you waste time going through multiple spreadsheets.

3. **Unnecessary Motion** - You can't find the information to complete a task. You can't remember where the correct

version of the file is located. Is it in your email, on your desktop or on a server? You spend a lot of time and wasted motion to find the right version.

4. **Waiting** - is inactivity while you're waiting for information or a response. You sent an email and you haven't gotten a timely response.

5. **Over production of information** - You have inaccurate data sources for your analysis. You continue to manipulate the data to match the result you want versus having a portal that has all your project information posted to it.

6. **Over processing** - is too many reviews. My coworker and I have different versions of the data (no single version of the truth) and spend time reviewing with multiple stakeholders.

7. **Defects** - is producing an incorrect analysis. I was sent the wrong version of the information to produce a report that resulted in the wrong decision being made.

8. **Wasting the intellectual resources of the team** - Not using my stakeholders in the analysis of problems and leveraging the wisdom of the team. This happens frequently due to the nature of using an asynchronous communication channel such as email or texting without using an effective communications process that creates collaboration within a team.

Knowledge workers inject waste into the process because they approach it from a "craft" approach versus a repeatable process approach. People are busy, interrupt driven and are usually skimming the surface, so you must have their attention when you're communicating. How many people do you know who will answer an email rapidly one day and then go into hibernation for the next email? Our world today has so many distractions that it's hard to keep your focus.

There's nothing like being on conference calls all day and being bombarded with instant messages, texts and emails while trying to pay attention to what's being discussed on the call. Using the *Five Simple Checklists* approach will simplify project management for you and help you deliver on your commitments.

Today, knowledge work has matured and is being distributed across the globe. Mass production is in place for Information Technology, Cloud Services, Customer Relationship Management (CRM), etc. with modular, reusable code and tools. You want to leverage the knowledge that adds value versus the knowledge that drives waste in your processes.

DELIVER THE BEST SERVICE TO YOUR CLIENTS BY:

- Use Lean Principles to eliminate waste
- Learn the discipline of project management
- Collaborate to maximize the capabilities across your teams
- Identify and address your risks

Project management is a complex task with many moving parts. How do you manage that complexity and deliver projects on time and within budget? The use of checklists and the significant quality improvements they yield are far-reaching and not tied to any one field or discipline.

CHAPTER 2
Core Principles

[A strong foundation is the pillar of success]

"THE MOST DANGEROUS KIND OF WASTE IS
THE WASTE WE DON'T RECOGNIZE."

- SHIGEO SHINGO

This chapter will give you the basic understanding of the four key principles that the *Five Simple Checklists* are built upon. Those principles are Lean, Standard Work, Eliminating Waste and Six Sigma.

Lean principles are about continuous improvement in your business using the framework that was originally developed in Japan and achieved notoriety known as the *Toyota Production System (TPS)*. Lean is focused on eliminating waste from your processes.

There are eight forms of waste that were discussed in Chapter 1 and we'll spend more time on them in this chapter.

Standard Work is defining the standard operating procedures that are used to perform work on a repeated basis. The focus is to eliminate variation in your processes, so they become repeatable and provide consistent results. Successful project managers deliver consistent results. The *Five Simple Checklists* are your roadmap to deliver standard work for projects that you manage.

Six Sigma is how you measure and count. It's not a new concept and has been around since the 1980's. Six Sigma is a methodology that packages tools and concepts into a clear and systematic roadmap for process improvement using the 'DMAIC' (Define, Measure, Analyze, Improve & Control) problem-solving methodology.

Lean is a framework that was developed and used by Toyota and was immortalized in the book *The Machine that Changed the World*. Using this approach with project management will help you deliver on your commitments. Using the *Five Simple Checklists* will guide your project to focus on the value-added activities and minimize the waste. You want to focus on delivering value to your customer in everything you do which is the basis for applying Lean to your efforts.

Knowledge is following the value chain to help your customers turn data and information into impactful knowledge to manage your projects.

Data = Facts

Information = Data + Context

Knowledge = Information + Judgement

Defining value is the activity that changes data into information or information into knowledge to meet the customer requirements. Non-value-added activity is the activity that takes time or resources but doesn't transform data; something the customer would not be willing to pay for if given the choice.

You are never defined by what you did for your customer yesterday, but what are you doing for them today. Are you going to deliver a future that will improve their business? Focus on today and how to make the future a reality. Forget about yesterday because you can only go forward, not in reverse.

Lean principles can be built into every project you manage. I've provided the *Five Simple Checklists* to be used as your roadmap to deliver outstanding results consistently and Lean principles have been incorporated throughout.

There are six Lean principles that you will apply. The first is to specify value to the customer. Using the *PSS Checklist* will provide the specification as you document the problem statement, develop the business case and create the *Day in the Life (DITL)* as the vision for the future. For Agile projects, you will specify the value through the user stories. The user stories must be well thought out and complete in order to be able to finish the project on time and on budget. The *APM Checklist* identifies steps to ensure this is accomplished.

The next step is to identify the value stream. The value stream for managing a project is delivered with completing your project on schedule. Using the *MYS Checklist* identifies the value stream for the project and if you're managing an Agile project, you will identify the value streams when you map the user stories to the sprints.

Creating flow to the customer by eliminating waste in the project management process is accomplished using the *PSS Checklist* to create the right framework, using the *MYS Checklist* to manage the project and the *CFS Checklist to* manage the change process in both traditional and Agile projects.

The next principle is to let the customer pull value. The customer is focused on the project completion. The one thing they want most is a current status and knowledge of progress or risks. To pull value means when they want to review it, not when you want to push it to them. It is key that you set up a collaboration space for the team and communications that will provide the information to your customer. The customer doesn't have to call you or send emails to find out what is going on with the project. You've created a space they can pull value from anytime they need to see an update.

The pursuit of perfection through continuous improvement is the final principle and one that the *Five Simple Checklists* will help you accomplish. You are following a standard work approach that provides a higher level of quality rather than an ad-hoc approach. You are also using the closing process, the *CPS Checklist*, to drive continuous improvement across the organization by using a "lessons learned" approach to identify improvements which can be incorporated into future projects.

A primary focus when applying Lean principles is to improve the efficiency of a process. You get efficiencies by eliminating waste in your processes and "mistake" proofing your processes. There are three types of waste in the Japanese production management systems:

Muda - Wasteful activity that obstructs smooth flow on any activity

Type I Muda - Any activity that adds no value, but is necessary to completing the value-added function

Type II Muda - Any activity that adds no value and can be eliminated without impact to the product

Mura - Any inconsistency in the system that is caused by a lack of standards and poor change control

Muri - The physical strain on production workers that is characterized by constant firefighting and repair; the strain on staff resources and the unrealized potential of staff and capabilities.

The same forms of waste that are present in a manufacturing environment are present in the office. As long as you have a process that is used to perform work, you can identify waste in it.

Traditional Waste	Examples of Waste – Manufacturing	Examples of Waste – Knowledge Workers
Too Much Inventory	Produced too much product so there are inventory write-offs, scrap, etc.	Too many reports, too many unfinished projects, too many emails in our inbox, etc.
Unnecessary Transportation	Moving material from one location without adding value to the product – Lack of organization and Lean work flow	Moving information from one location (file/spreadsheet) to another; moving data from one system to another to view in a different format or provide different reports.
Over Processing	Extra steps are taken to produce product. Too much testing/rework before completion.	Creating spreadsheets to analyze information rather than managing Master Data to standards.
Waiting – Queue Time	Waiting for inventory to be able to build product. Waiting for machine time due to backlog.	Waiting on results before taking action (integration/unit test), waiting on responses to emails.
Unnecessary Motion	Looking for tools and parts, picking up things to only set them back down, poor facility layout.	Too many reviews/meetings to rework priorities/conflicts/changes. Poor requirements and not managing stakeholder expectations.
Producing Defects	Excessive variation, additional inspection/repair resources, missed deadlines.	Poor change management process that increase downtime and reduce productivity.
Producing Too Much	Inventory stockpiles, build ahead of demand, extra storage locations/manpower.	Generating additional reports, additional data analysis due to poor requirements.
Injuries	Lost workdays, injured personnel, etc.	Unrealized Human Potential – Lost opportunities to perform work due to firefighting and constant priority changes.

For Lean, one of your keys to success is being able to obtain and deliver upper management support. You obtain this by creating a clear vision of the future and communicating it well. Effective project managers know how to tell a story and they don't tell it once; they communicate it over and over again until the story becomes real.

The next principle is to prepare and motivate people to achieve a connection and alignment with the project. You should strive for ownership with the team by creating a connection with the project. Using the *PSS Checklist*, you will develop a *Day in the Life (DITL)* and collaborate with your team so they have input into the process to create a shared vision. In the development of your action plan, the *DITL* will serve as your compass to achieve your project goals and as the basis for the "as-is" / "to be" gap analysis gap analysis.

The next step is to measure performance so that you know how you're performing. We will cover the critical performance metrics in Chapter 10 so that you can manage your schedule using the *MYS Checklist*. One of the issues I had as a young project manager was not having a good metric to articulate where I was on my schedule and budget. I was always on schedule until I wasn't. The *Schedule Performance Index (SPI)* and *Cost Performance Index (CPI)* provide a quantitative measure to keep you on track with your project. In Chapter 10, you'll see a detailed example of how to use these metrics.

In today's work environment, you can have your team be almost anywhere in the world to support your project especially if you are developing software. I have a firm I'm using right now, that uses this model. The team lives all over the world and they work together no matter if they are in the States, Europe or South

America. Having the right collaboration tools to support information sharing is critical to your success.

The next element is to reward your team with recognition for their efforts, but also allow them the freedom to deliver in a way that supports the team and gives them maximum flexibility. This approach must have clear accountability and deliverables, and when it does, it works really well.

Focus on continuous improvement with a passion and never be satisfied with what you did yesterday. Your story is built upon what you're doing right now and how you're going to shape the future.

As a leader, you will need to focus on adding value to the business. First, you must understand the current state. To understand the current state, you will need to be data driven and focus on using quantitative information to describe it. Every business has processes that can be quantified using cycle time to determine the total time from beginning to end for the process to complete.

You can determine the quality of the process, in terms of the error rate produced, when you complete it and define the unit cost. For example, take the simple business process of invoice creation for a professional services firm. I'll use an extreme example for a business that has manual processes to capture time.

To identify the cycle time, you would look at the time it takes to capture all the time charged by employees to a customer. You would have a review to make sure all charges were valid and include some time to correct those that had errors. You'll need to track the total time until the invoice is ready to send to the customer. You'll track your quality at the final review by how many invoices are correct and how many are rejected by the customer. Based on the total touch time by the different individuals in the process, you should be able to assign a unit cost to processing an invoice.

You can develop your vision for the future once you've diagrammed your current state and identified the waste in your processes. Once you have these two artifacts, you can complete a gap analysis between the "as-is" state and the "to be" vision for the future. The gap analysis should be focused around the three critical metrics I've outlined for cycle time, quality and unit cost.

The gaps can easily be aligned using those metrics. If you find something you feel works better, then use it and understand the root cause of the defect that is driving your critical metrics.

Once you've identified how to correct the root cause, create a plan that eliminates the issue from a people, process and technology perspective.

You need to organize the resources required to address the issue or better yet, appoint a resource who can run with the task. One of your primary goals is to communicate and motivate your team. You do that by having a clear plan, with a strategy for achieving the plan and giving your team the freedom to hit the target.

Execute the process and monitor it as you go forward using the Six Sigma model (Define, Measure, Analyze, Improve & Control) or the ISO model (Plan, Do, Act, Check). Develop people by giving them the environment to be successful. Teach them how to use the available tools to solve problems and give them the freedom to do their job without micro managing them.

Go to where the work is being performed and see how it affects the process and the environment. Many people get used to the problems and just accept that it's part of the job. It isn't!

I was leading a team in a discussion and we were talking about an invoice backlog and why it was occurring. We were in a conference room and no one had a good handle on the issue. I asked the group to go to where the work was being performed and we found that there were stacks of invoices on a table that no one was processing because they were working other issues. The invoice issue was the most important issue in Finance at that moment and by seeing the issue, the team took immediate action.

Six Sigma had its origins at Motorola, where product field failures were highly correlated to massive variation in their internal processes and quality level. Motorola began a manufacturing focused campaign to prevent defects by controlling and optimizing processes ultimately leading to their winning the Malcolm Baldrige Award. Six Sigma is focused on measuring variation in your processes and product quality. Some variation is found in every process and in everything we do.

Variation can be measured in multiple ways (Cycle Time, Defects, Cost, Customer Satisfaction, Sales, etc.). There are a number of tools that can be used to help you identify your variations in processes. Six Sigma isn't just for manufacturing and can be used to measure the variation in your invoicing process as well as your factory yield for a specific product.

Some of the tools used in Six Sigma are cause and effect diagramming, root cause analysis, 5 why's, affinity diagrams, and swim lane charts. There are many more that can be used, but these are some of the common ones that I use.

Six Sigma is all about measuring your performance and as you can see from the table, your sigma level can have a dramatic impact on your quality level.

3 Sigma	4 Sigma	5 Sigma	6 Sigma
93.32000	99.37900	99.97670	99.99966

For instance, if you achieved 99.9% capability, it would result in:

- 20,000 wrong drug prescriptions a year
- 107 incorrect medical procedures a day
- 18,322 pieces of mishandled mail an hour
- 2,000,000 documents lost by the IRS a year
- Unsafe drinking water for 1.5 minutes each day
- Two short or long landings at any major airport each day

To drive transformation for your project you need to look at the inputs that will flow into your project, leverage the *Five Simple Checklists*, use a *RACI matrix*, and document your processes with swim lanes to deliver your project on schedule. The *Five Simple Checklists* are your tools to deliver standard work that focuses on eliminating waste in your processes. Standard work and the value of it is illustrated using the Standard Pig example that will be discussed in Chapter 5 for the *PSS Checklist*.

Standard work delivers a higher level of quality due to using repeatable processes for project management being performed the same way across all projects. You can tell a person how to do something, you can provide written instructions on how to perform a task or you can create a visual and use written instructions to deliver a quality product using standard work.

Using the *Five Simple Checklists* throughout the project lifecycle will keep your project on schedule and improve the likelihood of effective communication with your key stakeholders so you can be successful.

CHAPTER 3
Avoid the Traps
[I assumed you knew]

"GOOD BUSINESS LEADERS CREATE A VISION,
ARTICULATE THE VISION, PASSIONATELY OWN THE
VISION, AND RELENTLESSLY DRIVE IT TO COMPLETION.

-JACK WELCH

There are three "traps" I see project managers fall into that drag down the efficiency and effectiveness of the project and the team. They are *Activity Without a Plan (AWP)*, *Don't Manage by Email (DME)* and *Customer Disconnect Again (CDA)*.

Let's start with *Activity Without a Plan (AWP)*. I've seen many projects start with people just doing something to get started without any planning. It's the shoot, ready, aim, fire approach that may provide an early win simply because some activity is being performed. Unfortunately, you will quickly find yourself in trouble because you didn't have a baseline, you didn't get an agreement on budget, deliverables and a defined schedule. All you are operating on is "fix this problem".

I realize the pressure to get a "quick win" can be significant at times, especially when your boss is breathing down your neck. Delivering has to have a balance and you definitely need to find a "quick win" that is tactical in many cases. This book provides many examples from developing checklists, applying standard work or using metrics to identify your critical business processes. You must have flexibility in your approach and use good business logic to address issues that may or may not have an impact on your project.

If you are a purist and can't make a compromise to satisfy a real issue, then you're probably not going to get a lot of value from this book. I want you to be successful and apply common sense to solving your complex problems.

Let's address *Don't manage by Email (DME)*. One of the issues I see in today's business world is that people believe they can manage projects by email without the heavy lifting needed with managing relationships, having interactions with your team and having problem solving discussions about the project. Email is very useful but can create more confusion in some cases.

Email was invented by Ray Tomlinson and was first used in the 1960's. By the mid 1970's email took on the characteristics of what we see today. It's still based on a store-and-forward model. The email servers accept, forward, deliver and store messages across computer networks. Today, we use the internet as the transport mechanism to be able to deliver to anyone with a valid email address. The email used in the 1970's and the email today hasn't changed significantly.

Of course, email works across multiple devices and platforms, but it's much less effective today than when it began. There is so much noise in the environment today, with social media, texting, notifications, etc. that you have a hard time paying attention to the tasks at hand. Email doesn't make that any easier because it's a push system and not a pull.

Push systems don't provide workflow or processes. How many times have you missed work for a few days due to vacation or illness and found yourself totally stressed due to the emails piling up without your response? Email drives down productivity and is one of the biggest examples of waste in the business community.

For example, how many times have you seen an email go out to a distribution list and the "Reply All" goes on forever. Back and forth, back and forth, with questions, some comments out of left field and other general remarks without a solution. Pick up the phone!!!! Better yet, go see the person who has the issue, but stop the insanity.

Email has been examined multiple times in an effort to identify a strategy or a process to help manage it with some level of sanity. Some people buy into the "process to zero" approach. Some companies have banned people from reading or responding to emails on a certain day of the week. For the most part, it's a "catch as catch can" approach that leaves everyone wondering how to manage the email monster.

Email is really about communications. People will hide behind email, abuse it, ignore it and "cherry pick" what they do read. The exception is the person who will read, respond and remember all emails. Very few people fit this profile and if they do, you have to wonder how effective it really is for their audience. Some people say they receive over one hundred emails each day and others claim to receive more. I find this usually exaggerated, just like stock market returns or the size of the fish that was caught but got away.

Using other technologies to collaborate as well as making time for the face to face meeting, phone calls or video is the path the effective project manager will follow. Slack is a very popular communications tool being used across companies and projects. It is a cloud-based set of proprietary team collaboration tools and servers.

You create a workspace for your team which will be a shared hub for members to communicate and collaborate. You can organize your views by channels, so it can be organized around departments, projects, physical locations, etc. This way you have a higher percentage of your communications that will be read and understood by your team members. Slack is an effective tool that is much better than email to communicate more effectively in a digital environment.

There are other tools that can be used as well. Microsoft teams is an example of another tool that is getting traction as Microsoft continues to build on the O365 ecosystem. Others are Bitrix24, Basecamp, Fuze, Glip, Monday.com, etc., but nothing substitutes for face to face communications. If you don't have relationships with the team, you need to find a way to build them, do it effectively and do it now.

Once you have relationships with the team, then you can better leverage the digital tools to meet your objectives. However, sometimes you can't afford the travel to bring people together and you'll need to build in efforts to cultivate relationships which will make people feel a part of the community and identify with the common goal. Developing a clear picture of the "to be" state is important if you're managing a project which will change the way work is done.

Using tools like a *Day in the Life (DITL)* to describe the future and the "as is" state can help teams rally around the vision. You can hold contests to have team members submit answers to questions in a live environment using a tool like Stage Tally that will provide feedback for you in a very effective manner. There are a variety of ways to build a team and you will need to find out what works best for you and your team.

Customer Disconnect Again (CDA) is a problem I've seen with project managers who start to get too comfortable in their job and start taking the customer for granted. It starts with losing your discipline on reporting and communication. Instead, you start using an ad-hoc approach to manage the communication since you've established a familiarity with the customer. Items that had been more formal when you were building the relationship have now started to be sporadic in frequency or have stopped altogether.

Your customer requires you to be proactive and keep them informed on the project. You can't show up for meetings without being prepared or finding out five minutes before the meeting that you didn't test a critical step and your demo isn't going to work. You can't stop meeting your Key Performance Indicators (KPI)'s and move to an informal approach to communicate how you're managing the project.

Maintaining customer satisfaction is something you must always focus on to keep the relationship and trust that you've developed. That's why you focus on the *CFS Checklist* and maintain the discipline to follow it so that you don't experience *CDA*.

CHAPTER 4
Five Simple Checklists
[Leveraging your Time]

"To the person who does not know where he wants to go there is no favorable wind."

-Seneca

If you follow the basics of any discipline, sport or profession, it's about executing on the basics and not getting caught up in the latest craze. The basics of project management are about creating a level of quality that is consistent and delivers repeatable results. Always focus on the basics because they build the foundation for you and as projects become more complex a solid foundation will remain strong.

I've found in most companies that becoming a project manager is more of a "trial by fire" versus a directed approach with training and mentoring. It's amazing how many companies that are providing project management services as a core part of their business model, fail to train or to invest in the basics for their staff. This book will fill that gap for most smaller companies that want to upgrade the level of quality and service they provide to their clients. Quality is about repeatability and consistency.

Using the *Five Simple Checklists* across your organization to provide that level of consistency will upgrade your project management skills and improve the level of quality that you deliver on a day to day basis. As a project manager, it's important to focus on areas that you can control and not waste your energy on things that are out of your control.

In the book, *The 7 Habits of Highly Effective People*, Stephen Covey writes about the concepts of the Circle of Concern and the Circle of Influence. The challenge with the Circle of Concern is that you can't do anything about concerns, you can only impact change through your Circle of Influence. Within the Circle of Influence, there is a Circle of Control where your influence has its greatest impact, and that's where you should spend your energy. Too many times I see project managers fail because they spend energy on things that are totally out of their control and they lose focus on the critical tasks that matter. A project manager always has to deal with and be aware of the Circle of Concern and the Circle of Influence.

LEVERAGE CHECKLISTS TO MANAGE
YOUR PROJECT SUCCESSFULLY

You were told about the *Triple Constraint* in Chapter 1. The balancing of these three elements, when fully understood by the project manager, allows for the precise planning, resourcing and execution of a project. At the end of the day, these are the key elements of a successful project and will determine whether or not you have delivered on your commitments for the project.

The first thing a project manager must do is verify that the project is well understood so that the complete assigned task can be accomplished. Using the *PSS Checklist* will mitigate risks and make sure you get started on the right path with your project.

PROJECT STARTUP STANDARDS (PSS)

The *PSS Checklist* is your key for getting started on the right foot with your project and to make sure you know what problem you are solving. You need to have a clear picture of what you're doing. The first thing a project manager must do is verify that the project is well understood so that the entire task can be assigned and then be completed. This must be documented so it is well defined and there is no ambiguity in the requested project. With any project, there is the customer/client, the doer/implementer and the key stakeholders that must come to agreement on the scope. The project should have a charter that defines the project and the work to be completed. When you don't document the problem statement, you will be at risk for scope creep and changes because you're relying on verbal agreements and varying memories. Once these have been outlined the team can develop a clear picture of the "to-be" state. This will add clarity to the project that may at times be unclear, especially in the "fog of war" which you will experience when the tasks seem overwhelming and communications break down.

COMMUNICATE FOR SUCCESS (CFS)

Communication is an area that many people overlook because they are focused on doing rather than making sure the team and the stakeholders have a clear picture of the project and the required activity. If there's any specific item that most project managers overlook, it's consistently following the communication plan.

The *CFS Checklist* supports the steps that are in the *PSS Checklist*. Your problem statement, your project charter, and the business case will be used to define your project. Another critical element is putting a matrix together that defines who is responsible, accountable, informed and consulted *(RACI)* within your team. Getting this agreement up front will serve you well throughout the lifecycle of your project.

Your schedule, deliverables and your budget are necessary artifacts for you to communicate effectively on your project. The *CFS Checklist* covers the critical actions, recurring meetings and project artifacts that you will use to communicate to your team.

As a project manager, you are responsible for keeping your project sold and building the credibility needed to maintain the support throughout the lifecycle.

I remember a project that was being managed by a member of my team who was hitting most of the milestones, but because the project manager communicated infrequently, the sponsor thought that the project was failing, and we needed a new project manager. Instead of replacing the project manager, we started meeting with the sponsor weekly to review progress and because we were executing, the sponsor eventually changed their perspective. Even when things are going well, if it's not communicated, you can still have a failure.

MANAGE YOUR SCHEDULE (MYS)

Managing the schedule is a core competency of project management and there is no excuse for a project manager to not be familiar with the details. In order to deliver commitments, you must have defined milestones and a specific due date associated with each milestone. The right metrics and approach are critical in order to be data driven in the management of your schedule. **Do not** operate by your "gut feelings".

Schedules change on a frequent basis and the project manager must make adjustments to maintain the overall schedule, even if some milestones don't hit their planned date. The schedule is dynamic and adjusting is a constant.

The depth and details on a project need to have a delicate balance to be of use in managing a project. One of the mistakes that I see, especially with first time project managers, is to incorporate too much detail into the project schedule. If you have so much detail in your schedule that you're changing things daily, then you've created an issue.

The best approach is to identify the most critical milestones and make sure they are tracked and updated. These milestones are the ones that would impact your project significantly if they were missed and would interfere with other tasks being completed.

AGILE PROJECT MANAGEMENT (APM)

The *APM Checklist* was developed to ensure that the process is being used in accordance with the Agile principles. In many cases, the Agile team is focused on doing versus making sure your team and stakeholders have a clear picture of the project and the activity. If there's any area that most project managers and/or the scrum master will overlook is, the communication. Many times, in an Agile development the team treats the exercise as a "black box". They go through the user stories, finish their sprints and things come out differently than what the customer thought when the project started. The communication that takes place must be timely and accurate to maintain the customer relationship.

Using the *CFS Checklist* as a guide will mitigate the communications issues that develop during a project. I've managed many vendors and internal teams on Agile projects. Most have their own approach that they have used over time and don't maintain the discipline needed to deliver quality products. The scrum master is the key role and if they follow the framework with discipline, a project manager will be redundant. Using the *APM Checklist* helps take away the ambiguity that might be in place if you're not following a repeatable process or your scrum master doesn't have the discipline needed.

Agile is an area where I've seen a lot of failures because people don't use the defined structure of Agile. The scrum master is the key to an Agile project and I've seen teams that don't have a scrum master or one that isn't disciplined in promoting and supporting the Scrum theory, practices, rules and values. I've added another step to ensure alignment, the *Day in the Life(DITL)* that tracks alignment with the original vision. If that changes, then the *DITL* should be updated to reflect the changes. I will discuss this in more detail in Chapter 5.

CLOSING PROJECTS SUCCESSFULLY (CPS)

Closing a project should be a celebratory event, but it's often skipped as everyone goes back to their full-time job or moves on to the next shiny object at work. You need to take these steps for your customer and the organization so that a continuous learning and improvement culture is built. The first step is to compare what you originally said you were going to do with what actually happened. These two will always be different, but if you've followed the *CFS Checklist* you should have the change logs that reflect what caused the variations.

You'll have a final team meeting to brainstorm lessons learned and develop the changes you'll need to continuously improve your project management skills in the organization. You may want to change the checklists for your unique needs or procedures in the organization that made it difficult to get things done. A critical part of effective project management is to be able to tell the story of the project and how things will be different. This can be accomplished through the *Day in the Life (DITL)*, example you'll see in Chapter 5.

After you've completed these steps, you'll document your findings in a report to your customer. The customer must have closure on both the results and the money that was invested to implement the project.

You will need to shut down any of the financial work orders that were used to fund and support the project. You'll then put together any sustainment plans that are needed to keep the project on track. This could be making sure that hardware/software costs that are required will be incorporated in the appropriate budgets as well as any human resources that are required for the ongoing support.

You've now closed the project and will send a note to the stake-holders outlining the results. And the final step is to have a celebration for the accomplishments. If it's a cake, a party or an after-hours event, have a celebration that recognizes the work and the people that made it happen. Take pictures and put them in your company newsletter so that employees will recognize the accomplishments and who participated.

You must have a sound plan and apply a process that is repeatable and applicable to any project, no matter the complexity or type. Following the *Five Simple Checklists* approach will save you time, frustration and money. If you follow the process, it will improve your ability to execute and deliver consistent, outstanding results.

I worked for a large company that made significant investments in the development, talent and tools necessary to manage projects effectively. They delivered large, complex projects that pushed the "edge" of current technology and delivered innovation to the cus-tomer. In several studies conducted that encompassed over 400 different projects, the data always pointed to the first 30 days as being critical to the success of the project. What happens in that time period that is so crucial?

You can't afford to play catch up and it is essential to get out in front of the effort. Trying to play catch up once you've started the race is not a winning strategy. You may get lucky, but then again you may not. You should understand what it means to have "buy-in" to support the successful delivery of your project. Just because you think you have authorization to proceed doesn't mean you'll be successful without real buy-in. You will fail if your stakeholders only give you "lip service" and have that passive aggressive behavior that can be common in many organizations. I've had that happen due to my urgency to move forward, meet the schedule and see progress. Unfortunately, it cost me political capital and impacted the project results.

Avoid the traps that so often contribute to the failure of the project in the first 30 days. For example, you never got your primary sponsor baseline documented, and now you are in a real bind. Depending upon your working relationship, you can get into the mode of dragging the rock in to the sponsor and it's never the right rock. I can't tell you how many times I've seen this and have been victim to it myself. I've conducted many post mortems on projects that didn't meet their objectives and *Activity Without a Plan (AWP)* is one of the top reasons projects fail. By the time you get into the project and realize you are way off target, you have spent too much money and burned too much schedule to go back and recover.

The common traps for failure as a project manager are:

ACTIVITY WITHOUT A PLAN (AWP)

This is one of the easiest traps to fall into because people want to see action and progress immediately. It feels good for the first 30 days, but you've sown the seeds of failure because you didn't understand the scope of the work, the schedule and key deliverables. You wouldn't want a builder to start your house without an architectural plan with dimensions, material specifications, a budget and a schedule, would you?

AWP creates chaos for many companies as failure becomes built into the project because you didn't follow the *PSS Checklist.*

When work isn't specified and documented, people often have different perspectives on what will actually be accomplished. The act of documenting the scope will bring clarity and purpose to your project. Otherwise, you'll be in the "bring me a rock" mode when your work isn't specified. Every day you bring a rock to the sponsor or client and it's the wrong type of rock; the result is rework and waste.

DON'T MANAGE BY EMAIL (DME) OR TEXTING

Email and texting certainly have their place, but to have them be your primary communications channel is going to cause issues on your project. Email is the definition of waste from a classical Lean approach since it's always a push to your inbox and you may or may not be ready to process it. There is a school of thought that says the only way to manage email is to use Process to Zero (PTZ) every day, of which maybe 2% of people do.

Email is an overused, and sometimes ineffective tool because you can't guarantee that everyone reads it, understands it, and agrees with the priority. My favorite is the Reply All selection where you will see 10 replies before people tire of it or you get an answer. If you see more than two Reply All responses, kill it with a conversation, meeting or phone call. Organizations should have very clear standards in place for using email so people can communicate effectively rather than have the chaos that lives in their inbox.

I've seen people try to manage everything through email and it's typically a disaster. There is no replacement for picking up the phone or going to see the person and having a face to face, real conversation. I wish the world was so simple that you could effectively communicate in a digital manner, but we're not quite there yet. There are some innovations like Slack, Microsoft Teams, etc. that improve the collaboration process, but there is no substitute for a face to face conversation. You need context and a richer dialogue to fully understand complex issues.

CUSTOMER DISCONNECT AGAIN (CDA)

You now have approval and you're off to the races focusing on your deliverables and managing your schedule. The problem is that nothing remains static or fixed in time. Things change, new information is discovered and with that your original target or scope may change, but too many times you don't validate changes with your customer.

Maybe you're concerned they'll want you to change something that impacts your cost or schedule. That may be the case, but you have to manage change in everything you do. Keeping your customer informed and "bought in" to the project is essential.

The customer must always be a focus in your efforts. Even if everything is going perfectly, which it rarely does, you still need to provide a regular communication to your client.

Many times, you'll have a disconnect because you stop communicating on a regular basis, or the project has some challenges and your sponsor starts to hear anecdotal comments about the project failing, etc. Don't let your sponsor hear things (bad news) in the hallway or via email. Bad news needs to come from you, so you can address the issues with a corrective action plan.

Own this and you'll be on your way to having a successful approach to managing projects. Don't own it and the communication gaps will be filled by people who may or may not know all the details.

REAL BUY IN (RBI)

The key to managing change is communications. Some project managers like to run their project like a "black box". You only see what goes into it and what comes out of it. I understand some of this mentality since if you're competent in your job, you may not feel like reviews and oversight add any value to your project.

Don't make this mistake because it will be deadly for you. Project manager maturity is critical when you're managing change. Your job is to make it easy on your sponsor and your team.

The best way to have *RBI* is to follow the *Five Simple Checklists* approach and pay particular attention to the *PSS* and *CFS Checklists*. These two checklists ensure a good baseline and consistent, ongoing communication that will make your project successful. Knowing what you're being asked to do and communicating it well will help you manage the change process so that your team and stakeholders have the information they need.

All projects have difficult issues that will be Human, Process or Technology related. I've seen project managers fail miserably on elements of their projects but communicate so well that the customer felt they were achieving the results needed.

Implement the *Five Simple Checklists* and avoid the traps that keep you from delivering outstanding results for your organization. Follow the roadmap I have outlined, and it will put you far ahead of most people and you will definitely stand out from the crowd. The *Five Simple Checklists* are designed so you can deliver project results in a repeatable manner and put your career on the right track to achieve your goals.

Delivering consistently is the definition of quality. If you have significant variations in your results you will have poor quality. Do you have a favorite restaurant that you go to with a wait person that you always use? Do they always greet you with a smile on their face and do they make you feel important? Their service enhances your meal and the experience that you have in the restaurant. Even if the food may not be as wonderful at it always is, the person that waits on you makes the experience worth going again. You patronize that restaurant for that reason because you know what to expect when you walk in. You need to be able to do the same when managing projects.

By using this approach your customers will know what to expect. Over time, avoiding the pitfalls will become easier and consistent performance with repeatable results with be the norm. You are able to define your process from start to finish and in doing so, people will buy in to your approach. The other approach is to run around all day with your hair on fire, going from crisis to crisis and at the end of the day you're exhausted. You go home, drink a bottle of wine, or two, then get up and go do it all over again. Avoid the traps and get your life back. Have a plan!

CHAPTER 5

Project Startup Standards (PSS) Checklist

[How you Start determines how you Finish]

ONE DAY ALICE CAME TO A FORK IN THE
ROAD AND SAW A CHESHIRE CAT IN A TREE.
"WHICH ROAD DO I TAKE?" SHE ASKED.
"THAT DEPENDS A GOOD DEAL ON WHERE YOU
WANT TO GET TO," SAID THE CAT.
"I DON'T MUCH CARE WHERE," SAID ALICE.
"THEN IT DOESN'T MATTER WHICH WAY
YOU WALK," SAID THE CAT.

-LEWIS CARROLL, ALICE IN WONDERLAND

The *Project Startup Standards (PSS) Checklist* is your key for getting started on the right foot with your project and to make sure you know what problem you are solving. The *PSS Checklist* was developed using the data from "lessons learned" that I documented from both successful and failed programs throughout my career.

Too many project managers depend upon informal direction, lack of scope definition and unclear roles and responsibilities. These project managers typically operate in a crisis mode therefore the project is rarely successful. The *PSS Checklist* is your initiating and planning stage for your project.

Taking the time to set up the necessary standards before starting a project is crucial for your success. You mitigate risks by addressing your standards up front and having a methodology and rhythm that creates discipline.

When you don't set standards and have a scope that is "soft", you will end up falling into the *Activity Without a Plan (AWP)* trap. As I discussed earlier, this is one of the easiest traps to fall into because people want to see activity immediately. Never confuse activity with progress.

Steps for PSS Checklist	Complete Y/N
Problem statement documented and validated	
Executive Support obtained and a primary sponsor identified	
Project Scope/Charter defined/documented (specify the work)	
Stakeholders Identified	
Document the current overall process in a swim lane	
Create a Day in the Life for the future state when the project is complete/implemented	
Business Case Completed with Critical Characteristics identified (Quality, Unit Costs, Cycle Time)	
Complete a *RACI* for the team	
Develop the schedule and deliverables	
Develop risk register and mitigation plans	
Project Scope and Costs documented	
Funding Allocated/Budgeted	
Identify and select a collaboration tool	
Kick off meeting and document meeting results	

WRITE THE PROBLEM STATEMENT DOWN!

Whether you're a first-time project manager or a veteran, the first thing you need to do when you're given an assignment is to write down the problem statement. Too many times, I've been given direction to go solve the problem with verbal inputs. Just make it happen! Too many project managers depend on informal direction and as informal input goes, the next day, there might be more information that may or may not agree with what I was first told. The *PSS Checklist* solves that problem with a standardized approach that will get you started on the right path and set the tone for your project.

Writing something down is powerful in so many ways because it forces you to think through the issue and when you put it to paper, it becomes clear. Once you've done that, you will need to review it with your sponsor and make sure they agree with it. It needs to be clear in terms of the problem with quantitative descriptions.

For example, our invoicing takes 30 days from the time we collect our labor charges and bill the customer. This creates significant issues for our cash flow and impacts our profitability by 10 percentage points. This delay also creates customer satisfaction issues for our clients because they are waiting so long to get the bill that they aren't sure what work was done once they get it. This results in an additional 20-day delay in getting paid.

The next step after documenting the problem statement will be to make sure you have executive support and a primary sponsor. This step requires you to put a communication together for the sponsor to send to the team stating definition of the project, the schedule and your role as the project manager. The sponsor will then send the communication out to the appropriate stakeholders in the organization. If you can't get agreement for this step, then you need to question whether this is something that can be supported in the organization and reassess the viability of the project.

Once you've gotten agreement from your sponsor and the communication has been distributed, then you need to develop the more formal scope and charter for the team that will be assigned to work with you for accomplishing the task.

The project charter should be developed as a team exercise if possible so that everyone participates in this event. This will specify the work to be completed based on the problem statement definition. Having a project charter will help you maintain the scope of the project and identify when you start to see *scope creep*. Every project has *scope creep* and you must have a process that you can use to manage change for your project. In addition, you'll sometimes get team members that want to add scope because it solves a problem for them or eliminates a pain point. You need a clear scope that can be used to keep everyone on the "same page". You will include the objectives of the project, the scope, project timeline, the dates for the effort, the project sponsors, the project manager, the core team members and the management review team.

The next item on the *PSS Checklist* is to document the current process in a swim lane format so that you can communicate the current "as-is" state. A swim lane diagram is used in process flow diagrams, or flowcharts, that visually distinguishes job sharing and responsibilities for sub-processes of a business process. Swim lanes may be arranged either horizontally or vertically. A swim lane chart is a lot like a flow chart, except it's primarily organized using organizations/functions and the processes being used. You can see the overall process on a single sheet of paper and that's helpful as you look to develop your new "to be" state. An example is provided below:

Customer	Defective Product				Ships product back to Vendor	Receives New Product
Customer Service			Trouble Shoot Problem	Verifies Source of Purchase	Generates RMA	Checks Inventory Balance
Warehouse				Receives Product	Inspects Product	Dispositions Product
3PL		Ships Product				
Finance			Tracks RMA's	Reconciles Credit Memos		

The next step that I use is to create a *Day in The Life (DITL)* describing how it will be different once you've solved the problem. I like to describe the "as-is" state and describe how it's different after you've implemented the changes. I captured these key elements as an example from a Salesforce implementation for a Private Equity Portfolio company which included the following:

The Problem Statement captured the "as-is" process being used and included the following:

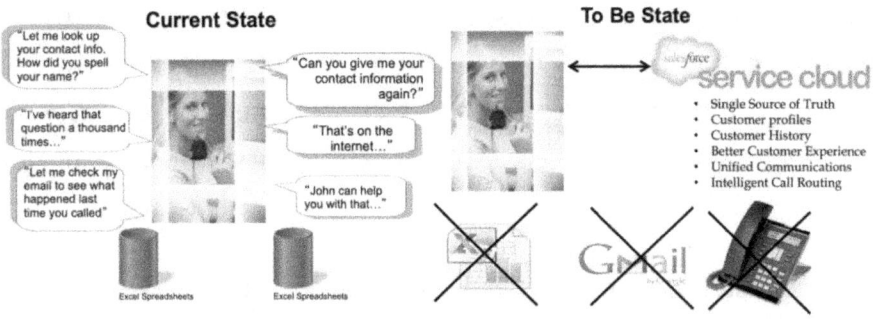

While it's not always required, I like to develop a business case for the project to determine the actual business value of completing the project. The key elements I focus on are defining the quality, unit costs and cycle times. In the case with the Salesforce implementation, the quality was related to the customer call and if the customer's concern could be resolved on the First Call. First Call Resolution (FCR) in this case was at 64%. Only 6 out of 10 customers that called would receive their answer. However, the other 4 customers would either be transferred or need a follow up that would generate another call.

In addition, we tracked the Average Handle Time (AHT) for the call which drove the number of calls we could answer. We had an AHT of over 8 minutes which translated in a cost per call of $20. Customer satisfaction was another factor because while the customer service representatives were awesome, they didn't have access to the data that would have rapidly resolved the customer's issue.

The business case was based on reducing the AHT and the cost per call. The other opportunities for improvement were to improve FCR and customer satisfaction. The by-product with this focus was to reduce customer wait times, and abandoned calls.

The next step is to develop a *RACI matrix* for the team and the participants that will be involved in the project.

Know your stakeholders, determine their role and obtain buy-in to guide your project. One of the biggest failure points in project management is not having agreement and buy-in. After making sure the scope/definition is well defined and agreed upon, the next biggest failure points occur in communication and project execution.

In today's work environment where email is used as the primary communication tool, you must focus on effective communication with your stakeholders. It is critical to know who is accountable for execution. Project members must understand their role, agree to it and then be held accountable for the completion of their tasks. The *RACI matrix* is a good tool to use to make sure people are engaged and understand what role they play in supporting the effort.

There are usually 4 types of people that you will see on your projects:

Action Angela – This person wants to take on too much and not stay in their swim lane and creates angst among the team.

Forgetful Frank – He's on distribution for everything but will sit in status meetings and claim that he wasn't included or didn't get the information he needed to do his job.

Always Late Louie – You always have to chase Louie down and get the latest status. He has trouble managing multiple priorities.

Steady Sandra – She always delivers on commitments and sets the standard.

RACI DEFINITIONS

Responsible - People or stakeholders who are the "doers" of the work. They must complete the task or objective or make the decision. Several people can be jointly responsible.

Accountable - Person or stakeholder who is the "owner" of the work. He or she must sign off or approve when the task, objective or decision is complete. This person must make sure that responsibilities are assigned in the matrix for all related activities. Success requires that there is only one person accountable, which means that "the buck stops here. "

Consulted - People or stakeholders who need to give input before the work can be done and signed-off on. These people are "in the loop" and are active participants.

Informed - People or stakeholders who need to be kept "in the loop." They need updates on progress or decisions, but they do not need to be formally consulted, nor do they contribute directly to the task or decision.

A *RACI matrix* is one tool that will help you manage projects effectively and drive accountability to the organization. Making sure that your team understands who delivers is a critical upfront step for any project manager.

The *RACI matrix* will take away the assumptions of who does what and will help put accountability in place as you go through the lifecycle of your project. You don't want Angela getting out of her swim lane.

THE BEST APPROACH IS TO MEET WITH YOUR KEY PROJECT MEMBERS AND DO THE FOLLOWING:

- Identify the roles in the project team
- List the key milestones and deliverables for the project
- Provide post it notes to each member and go through each deliverable. Ask the team to identify who is responsible and what role they play on the post it notes
- Collect the notes and put them on the wall to see if there are different perspectives
- When the team isn't aligned, and people have different opinions, discuss as a group

- Reach an agreed upon matrix and the discussions should uncover any issues that you need to pay attention to as you manage the project

Stephen Covey described it so well in his *7 Habits for Highly Effective People* when he talked about "Fast is Slow" and "Slow is Fast". As a young project manager, I didn't understand this completely but recognized the significance as I gained more experience managing projects and people. The buy-in process requires a time investment, and everyone needs to participate in it. Many times, I wanted to force decisions and move on to the next step. I was in a hurry and didn't believe that people needed to take up time discussing issues that I thought had no relevance. Everyone doesn't learn the same way and when I finally understood what Stephen Covey was saying, it made so much more sense to me.

On many issues you will need to work through the discussion with the team to make sure you have a clear understanding of the context. You can't always just drive to a decision quickly when it's complex and has multiple stakeholders, each with their own perspective. You need to take the necessary time for people to make sure there is a universal understanding of the project or problem. You want to minimize any misunderstandings and assumptions that can derail the project.

The key items to address are the following:

- Have the team walk through the matrix and discuss the roles and their responsibilities. This is critical to ensure the organization and the associated resources understand their roles

- Obtain agreement on *RACI* with the team
- Communicate the roles to your management team
- Obtain "buy-in" to the process

Topic / Activity	Development staff	Finance - Budget	Customer Service	Manufacturing - Receiving	Manufacturing	Manufacturing - Returns	Quality	IT	Sales	Call Center	Integration Partner	Primary Sponsor	Executive Support
Develop Charter	R	R	R	R	R	R	R	A	R	R	R	R	I
Develop Scope of Work	I			I	R	I	R	C		A	C		
Develop the WBS for the Project					R					C	A	C	
Identify Vendors Needed to perform work		R			R		R			C	A	I	
Develop Performance Baseline	C	R	C		C	R	C	R	C	C	A	I	
Identify Team Members					A					I	C		
Kickoff Meeting for the project					A						R		
Develop Scripts for testing key processes					R/A					I	C		
Data Migration					R					C	A	I	
System Architecture					R					C	A	C	
Define procurement needs	C		C		C	R	C		C		A	C	C
Procure needed resources			C		A					C	R	I	
Identify Risks and develop mitigations		C			A			C	C	R	C	I	
Develop Vendor integrations	C		C		C	C	C		C		A	R	
Setup Test environment	I	R	I		I	C	I	R	I	C	A	I	I
Data migration to test	I	C	I		I	C	I	C	I	C	R/A	I	
Execute test scripts and scenarios	I	C	I		I	C	I	C	I	C	R/A	I	I
Monitor project	I			I			I		I	C	R/A	I	I
Identify and communicate risks and obstacles					R			C	I		A	C	
Identify and communicate resource needs					C				C	C	R/A	C	
Operational Readiness Review					C						R	A	
Approve test results					C						R	A	
Approve Implementation					C						R	A	

R = Responsible (does the work, makes the decisions)
A = Accountable (has final responsibility and often approves decisions and products
C = Consulted (provides input)
I = Informed (is told of outcomes)

Much of the schedule development will come out of the charter design process with the project team. You'll need to take that and move it into a tool that you can you use to maintain the schedule, make changes and perform any analysis needed from a task perspective.

Identify the risks that can impact your project. Develop the risk register and mitigation plans. The risk register is a document that contains information about identified project risks, analysis of risk severity and evaluations of the possible solutions to be applied. Presenting this in a spreadsheet is often the easiest way to manage things, so that key information can be found and applied quickly and easily. If the risk is realized during the project, mitigation plans identify the corrective action to take.

Once you've developed a schedule, understand the task durations and understand the types of resources that will be applied, then you will be able to develop your project costs for implementation. I use a *Work Breakdown Structure (WBS)* or a mind mapping tool to break down the activity and estimate it. Now, you must obtain the funding to support the activity. This is critical to document and make sure you have the support to move forward. In some cases, you will not get the budget you requested, and you'll have to adjust by reducing scope, replacing resources with lower cost resources or extending the timeline. Remember the *Triple Constraint* that we explored earlier.

One of my first project management assignments involved the consolidation of all the distributed computing resources for Martin Marietta after they purchased General Electric Aerospace. This was in the early 90's and we still had a significant number of minicomputers that were used primarily to support engineering analysis and design. The Digital Equipment Corporation (DEC) was entrenched in the engineering community and disappeared in what seems like a very short time. DEC failed to acclimate to the transformation driven by the introduction of the Engineering Work Stations in the development of electrical and mechanical designs. Disruption happens frequently in the technology industry.

These workstations made it possible to deploy to individual designers at a fraction of the cost of the minicomputers. These companies didn't recognize the disruption that occurred when the economics for workstations changed and they didn't respond rapidly.

The primary goal of the project was to save $140,000,000 over a five-year period to meet the cost reduction targets. Our efforts were to:

- Consolidate the help desks
- Consolidate telecommunication contracts and renegotiate based on increased volumes
- Consolidate organizational responsibilities
- Consolidate the scientific computing centers
- Rationalize the facilities across the company

The other challenge we had was including virtual teams across the United States that had not worked together before or even met face to face. This would make interacting problematic given the different cultures and locations. We didn't have the collaboration tools that are in place today, making communications even more arduous.

It was early in my career and I had never managed a project this large and complex. I was a little intimidated by the task, but I had some very senior people who helped me and provided me the benefit of their experience. It helped me to develop some of the tools and approaches that I still use today when managing projects across multiple locations.

I had several takeaways from this assignment, and I've listed two that should be included in every project you manage:

First, manage the total project, tracking your current milestones and the ones that are behind schedule. I use the following categories:

- Planned milestones by week
- Milestones completed by week
- Milestones missed by week
- Burn down plan
- Total cumulative planned for each week
- Total cumulative completed by week
- Total cumulative missed by week

Using these categories and tracking them each week will provide you with a clear status which shows your progress at a glance. Your early warning system is when the cumulative missed by week exceeds 10% of your total planned by week.

I color code my project based on overall progress. I want to know how I'm progressing each week and will color code the schedule based on a Red/Yellow/Green rating. The definitions I use are:

Red – The project will not meet the intended scope and you cannot recover the schedule to meet the original plan

Yellow – I'm trending in the wrong direction, but have a "credible" plan to recover and still meet the intended scope in the required time

Green – On track to meet scope based on the specified schedule

Here is an example of a simple spreadsheet that I use for managing the resources and milestones, so I have a clear one-page perspective on the progress.

	Week 1	Week 2	Week 3	Week 4	Week 5	Week 6	Week 7	Week 8
Resource 1 Planned Hours	20	20	25	25	25	30	30	20
Resource 2 Planned Hours	15	10	10	15	15	25	25	10
Resource 3 Planned Hours	10	10	10	20	20	20	25	20
Resource 1 Actual Hours	15	15	20	25	15	35	20	25
Resource 2 Actual Hours	15	10	10	10	15	30	25	20
Resource 3 Actual Hours	15	10	10	20	20	30	25	15
Total Hrs Planned by Week	45	40	45	60	60	75	80	50
Total Hours Worked by Week	45	35	40	55	50	95	70	60
Total Cumulative Delta	0	-5	-10	-15	-25	-5	-15	-5
Planned Milestones by Week	4	6	8	8	10	12	10	8
Milestones Made by Week	2	4	5	5	8	10	12	10
Milestones Missed by Week	-2	-2	-3	-3	-2	-2	2	2
Total Cumulative Planned Milestones	4	10	18	26	36	48	58	66
Total Cumulative Milestones Made	2	6	11	16	24	34	46	56
Total Cumulative Milestones Missed	-2	-4	-7	-10	-12	-14	-12	-10
Resource Status (R/Y/G)	G	G	Y	Y	Y	Y	Y	Y
Milestone Status(R/Y/G)	G	G	Y	Y	Y	Y	Y	Y

Second, you will need to develop a clear vision for where you are going and a one-page summary of your end state. This is the *Day in the Life (DITL)* vision that will be your guiding light for the project.

For the *DITL* example, there was a company actively acquiring prospective companies to scale and grow the business but were not integrating the financials rapidly or efficiently. They were always behind, the people were stressed, and they were not delivering quality results. I use the "hair on fire" analogy again, where every day, you come into the office, pour a can of accelerant on your head, light it and run around trying to put it out all day.

They operated in a true interrupt driven environment that produced inconsistent results. At the end of the day, they would pour a bucket of water on their head to put out the fire, walk out of the office dazed and go home depleted.

The company acquisitions were not going to stop as scale was critical to their business model and continued year after year because growth drove the multiple of the stock. Their processes were highly variable, people didn't follow a defined process and the result was poor quality (inconsistent results, increased cycle time for the integrations and more pressure to solve the problems).

I used a Kaizen approach to help this client start addressing the issues in a way that would put them on a path to improve their quality, reduce their costs and cycle time. A Kaizen is a continuous improvement approach that uses many Lean tools to solve problems. As a part of that effort, the team created a vision that would guide them in their journey to solve this problem. Having a clear picture of the current "as-is" state and the new improved "to be" state is critical to getting people on the same page as well as communicating with your sponsors.

To start your brainstorming process, you'll ask your team questions like:

Imagine what things would be like if we stopped:

- Having customer returns
- Having to rework our invoices to contain accurate and timely information
- Having to reboot our systems when things stop working

Imagine what things would be like if:

- Our customers were our best advertising source and social media was used to sing our praises versus "hate on" our service.
- Everyone focused on solving the customer's issue versus following a corporate procedure that makes no sense and frustrates the customer.
- We were able to focus on continuous improvement and mistake proofing our processes.

Lofty goals require a clear vision for the future. You must have a clear vision that people can use to see that things will get better and their jobs will become more fulfilling. A higher level of job satisfaction will translate into more customers.

If you don't communicate this clearly, you are leaving it up to everyone else to define what your project will accomplish. You want to compare and contrast your current state with how things will be different once you implement the changes. Having a picture that describes the process will help you continue to keep your project focused on the future state.

An example *DITL* chart describes the current "as-is" state and the new "to-be" state that you want to achieve.

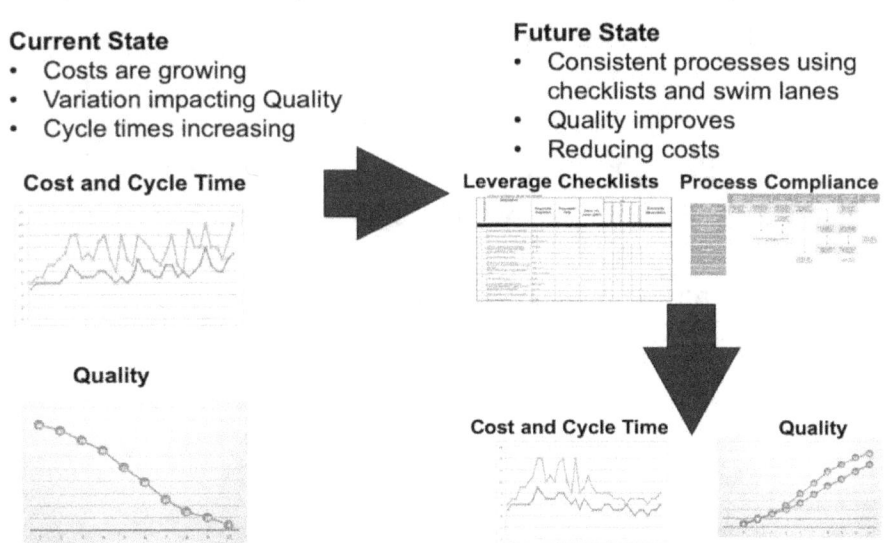

The transformation plan vision aligns the message as well as the actions the team will take to improve quality, reduce costs and deliver standard work. Standard work is the key to quality and many organizations don't really understand the concept. When leading a Kaizen event, we use an example known as *Standard Pig*. *Standard Pig* is a Lean simulation to demonstrate a Lean approach to delivering standard work. This simulation crystalizes the concept of standard work with the team in a way that is very powerful. When I use this exercise it's as if the light bulb goes off for all the people who were wondering why we were talking about standard work.

It uses the following steps to illustrate the value of standard work.

Ask the participants to draw a picture of a pig free hand without detailed instructions on how to draw the pig. As you would expect, everyone draws a different picture of the pig.

The second exercise provides detailed verbal instructions on how to draw the pig. The results are more consistent, but still have a high degree of variability across the drawings of the pig.

The final exercise provides detailed written instructions as well as a picture of the pig. This yields a much more consistent picture of the pig across the group.

Round 1

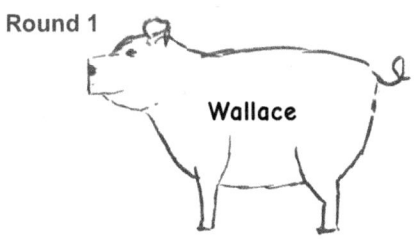

Wallace

Round 2

Standard Operating Procedure		Status Final
Standardize Work Instruction		Revision 1
		Rev. Date 8/29/2007
Procedure Number PIG0001-A		Page 1 of 1

Task	Description	Sub-Task	Instructions
1	Draw a letter M at the top left intersection.	1.1	Bottom center of M touches intersection
2	Draw letter W at bottom left intersection	2.1	Top center of W touches intersection
3	Draw letter W at bottom right intersection	3.1	Top center of W touches intersection
4	Draw arc from letter M to top right intersection		
5	Draw another arc from top right intersection to bottom right W		
6	Draw an arc between the two bottom Ws		
7	Draw the letter O in center left box		
8	Draw arc from letter M to tangent of the circle		
9	Draw arc from left W to tangent of the circle		
10	Draw an arc for the mouth	10.1	Half way between the W and circle
		10.2	Must be a happy pig
11	Draw an arc for the eyes	11.1	Half way between the M and circle
12	Draw cursive letter e near top of arc on right		
13	Draw two dots in middle of circle for pigs' nose.		

Round 3

Standard Operating Procedure		Status Final
Standardize Work Instruction		Revision 2
		Rev. Date 8/29/2007
Procedure Number PIG0001-A		Page 1 of 1

Task	Description	Sub-Task	Instructions
1	Draw a letter M at the top left intersection	1.1	Bottom center of M touches intersection
2	Draw letter W at bottom left intersection	2.1	Top center of W touches intersection
3	Draw letter W at bottom right intersection	3.1	Top center of W touches intersection
4	Draw arc from letter M to top right intersection		
5	Draw another arc from top right intersection to bottom right W		
6	Draw an arc between the two bottom Ws		
7	Draw the letter O in center left box		
8	Draw arc from letter M to tangent of the circle		
9	Draw arc from left W to tangent of the circle		
10	Draw an arc for the mouth	10.1	Half way between the W and circle
		10.2	Must be a happy pig
11	Draw an arc for the eyes	11.1	Half way between the M and circle
12	Draw cursive letter e near top of arc on right		
13	Draw two dots in middle of circle for pigs' nose.		

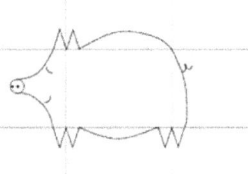

81

When working with team members across the company and possibly with outside vendors, being a *data driven* project manager who uses a standard work approach like the one demonstrated in the *Standard Pig* example will drive positive results.

The final step in the *PSS Checklist* is to have a kickoff meeting with the project team and the sponsors to go through the scope, charter, *DITL*, business case, *RACI*, risk register and the budget allocation. You should document the results, action items and schedule the next session using the *CFS Checklist* as your guide.

The seeds of failure are sown in the first 30 days for most projects. Focus on what you can control and execute on those tasks. Don't worry about all the things that are out of your control and distract you from the task at hand. You'll run across people who want to worry about things that make absolutely no difference and they will want to distract the team by having a discussion on something you can't do anything about.

Follow the *PSS Checklist* to mitigate your risks and set yourself up for success.

CHAPTER 6
Project Buy-In
[Avoid the Buzz Saw]

As I look back on my career, my checklist approach began when I developed the concept, strategy and project plan for a large information security project that would take over two years to finish and cost $60M+ to complete.

One of my biggest issues on that project was a lack of real buy in from some of the key stakeholders. We had that issue because there were five different companies (business areas) operating under one umbrella and each business area ran information security their own way. Each business area used different tools, different processes, and had different goals to meet the needs of their own business. In a company this size everything had a political component to it and this project was an 11 on a scale of 10.

When you have a company that's interconnected in a single network and everyone has their own toolset and processes you are going to have issues. We had a network design issue that compounded the problem since you could access any part of the unclassified network due to not having the proper segmentation and controls. You must have consistency across your processes and tools if you're running a large enterprise with a flat network and want interoperability. Without consistency and standards, you have a great deal of variation that drives your cycle time, quality and costs.

My failure to obtain that buy-in caused significant pain for me personally and impacted the speed at which we were able to move the project forward on a path to protect our corporation. The project was initiated due to some of the issues in our service delivery model for information security that started in 1999. The Melissa virus had spread through our network creating havoc as we applied the remediation, patches and network changes to address the issues. We were essentially five separate companies that did things differently to manage our infrastructure and information security. As an additional challenge , we were all connected to a single flat network. The next three years had repeated incidents across the company that required an intense focus to constantly remediate and address the issues.

Compared to today, the intrusions we were addressing were not complex, but due to our structure around people, processes and technology, we were constantly chasing a ghost. You could never achieve 100% remediation since the cycle times were so long to apply the patches and remediate the environment.

Even on the desktops, it would take 70+ days to install the updates and of course you had another update coming out before the current patch was applied. Granted, those same issues don't exist at the same level today due to the automation and tools that are in place today. The issues that exist today require greater vigilance, since the threats are much more sophisticated and damaging than ever before.

During this period, we started seeing what is known as the *Advanced Persistent Threat (APT). APT* is a state sponsored hacking usually performed by state sponsored entities like China, Iran, North Korea and Russia. These countries want to steal the Intellectual Property and Technology from the Defense Industrial Complex. Ever wonder why China's J-20 Fighters look a lot like our F-35 Fighters?

The hacking has become much more advanced now than it was then with tools developed specifically to vacuum all the data from your systems and export it to the hacker.

From 1999 to 2003 we were hit with these random acts of kindness on a regular basis. We didn't deal with the root cause but focused on the firefighting aspect. We had Emergency Action procedures, escalations for the incidents, communications that went out to all stakeholders, and a generally chaotic environment.

In the late nineties, in preparation for the Y2K issue that had everyone freaked out, we consolidated all our email systems to a common system from a combination of over 40 separate email systems. While the email consolidation created a lot of benefits, it increased our vulnerabilities across 130,000 desktops that were connected via email. Our company had put in place a central nervous system that allowed you to get to any location in the company due to a consolidated network and email system.

I had the assignment to pull together a project that would address the issue from an enterprise approach. Previously, I had implemented a Lean Six Sigma initiative across one of our largest divisions that had great success by significantly reducing cycle time, reducing costs, improving security and improving our quality for the same infrastructure services required at the enterprise level.

The new effort required many of the same elements that I had used in the Lean Six Sigma initiative to drive a complex project across multiple locations. We developed a vision of the "to be" state for what the change would mean for the business. We developed a real focus on the quality of the services being delivered and the cycle time reductions that were put in place as a result of the initiatives. I carried these items forward to the new project with the belief that this would be the right approach to deliver on the new challenge.

During this time, I put a team together that would support the execution of the project. Part of that team included a project manager that my boss wanted me to assign to the project to facilitate a growth opportunity for that individual. Part of a successful project is to make sure you have the alignment across your team to support the objectives of the project. An important part of that alignment is creating the vision necessary to understand the "to-be" state.

In the *PSS Checklist*, you'll see the step to create a *Day in the Life (DITL)* that shapes the vision. Through that process, you'll flush out any issues with the team that are important to address before heading down the wrong path.

During this phase of the project, I drafted resources needed to fill the critical openings. The project manager that was assigned to me, wasn't the right fit from a technical or strategic perspective. We clashed over the approach, the methods to achieve the objectives of the project and the vision that was in the *DITL*. I spent several months trying to balance the perspectives, but in the end, I had to make the decision to remove the project manager. As a result, I had to step in to fill the spot since we had lost valuable time.

Now, I'm pushing to make up for lost time and recover schedule from all the fallout caused by the six months we had spent screwing around with our approach and trying to achieve 'buy-in' with the business areas. There were five separate business areas, each with their own Chief Information Officer (CIO) that ran the

Information Technology (IT) organization to support their business area. The business areas viewed the Corporate CIO office where I worked about the same as you would view the government, when they said, "We're here to help". Skeptical would have been an understatement.

I had a good foundation for the technical execution of the project and the critical success factors to manage the project. We had a solid technical approach and were making progress, but in large organizations there are many dynamics at play, especially in the political space. We were doing what was necessary from an enterprise perspective to protect the corporation, but we didn't have the agreement with the business areas who wanted to maintain control of their individual organizations.

I didn't have all of the checklists needed to be successful in my endeavor and ended up hitting a "buzz saw". Relationships always matter, and you must have a good process to make sure you have agreements that people will honor. Just because everyone shakes their head "yes" in a meeting doesn't mean you have buy-in. You must put together enough of the structure, and have the artifacts in place, so that when you go around the room and ask the specific questions, you can get agreement. Once you get an agreement, you're not done, because you constantly have to maintain it.

The *CFS Checklist* was developed to mitigate the risks of hitting a "buzz saw". I developed numerous business cases due to the significant investment required to push the project forward. If the project was going to cost the business areas one nickel more, they were very resistant to fund the project. This went on for six months and finally, we got approval from the Corporate CIO for a significant portion of the project. I thought this was a tremendous win for the project. Unfortunately, I learned it was not as the events played out over the next twelve months.

I was told to push forward by the Corporate CIO and his CFO. They said, "Don't worry about the business areas", and I pushed forward with a renewed focus. What I didn't know was that the Corporate CIO would not commit or really support the project in the meetings that I did not attend. He was playing a political game and was hesitant to make decisions on funding. I became Darth Vader to some of the stakeholders since I was driving the project forward.

I owned the problem, and my actions drove some of the issues, but in a large organization with a complex matrix you move exceedingly slow, so sometimes you have to break a little glass to force issues that need to be addressed. You pay a price when you do that, but if you don't, you can end up with a project that never accomplishes anything and costs a lot of money. I have seen projects that would get into this state, spend a lot of money and never deliver any product.

I've used Stephen Covey's saying earlier as a reference on how, "Fast is Slow" and "Slow is Fast". This project made it really hit home for me. When I finally realized the issue, I went to each of the business area CIO's individually to see if I could salvage the relationships.

The last straw was when I visited the biggest critic of the project. I wanted to see if I could find out what I needed to do differently and rebuild the relationship, and he started yelling at me.

I had some success with all the business area CIO's except this one and I knew after the yelling match, that I couldn't salvage the relationship. I spent many nights thinking about how to solve the problem. I knew now I couldn't be successful as the "face" of the project no matter what I did. This project was critical for the corporation and I knew it could be done, but I could no longer be the face since I had become Darth Vader.

I hired a project manager who would become the face of the project and was great at building relationships. I also hired an outstanding deputy project manager that was well versed in managing the technical aspects of the project and would fill in the gaps necessary to manage a large, complex project like this. I wouldn't let either of these new managers become Darth Vader.

The project spanned two years and cost millions of dollars, but in the end, the project was hugely successful. My project manager did an amazing job. She built the relationships and the project succeeded in building the foundation for security to protect the corporation and reduce the labor that was required to support information security practices through common tools and processes.

There was a lot of "scar tissue" created from this experience and it's something that I carried forward to later efforts to learn from my mistakes. It doesn't matter what your boss or your sponsor says in private, it matters what they do in public. Look for clues and pay attention to the key elements that you must have in place to deliver on expectations.

The issues were a lack of an agreed upon scope and different expectations on the part of each stakeholder. My education from this experience, resulted in the checklist that I use to work communication and buy-in across stakeholders.

The *CFS Checklist* will be a critical part of your success since relationships always matter. Now, I really understand Stephen Covey's "Fast is Slow" and "Slow is Fast" so much better. It's easy and natural to want to force issues to get an answer to a problem. I recall early in my career talking to a mentor and his advice was that sometimes issues will take care of themselves without you having to step in and solve the problem.

My patience is always a little on the "thin" side and the *CFS Checklist* is a good reminder for me to make sure I'm staying on track. If you don't want your project to hit a "buzz saw", then you need to focus on effective communications and maintain your focus.

Sound project management is built on several key elements that should flow through the lifecycle of your project. I've learned these lessons after 30 years of managing hundreds of projects and making my share of mistakes.

The items to avoid are:

- Communication break down with the client
- Scope change not being addressed
- Schedules not reflecting reality
- Budget overruns
- Stakeholders not engaged and not understanding their roles

Let's focus on the critical elements that will help you achieve the "buy-in" you need to be successful. First, you must address the relationship management aspect of the project. Do you know your key stakeholders, and do you have a relationship with them? Have you gotten the support of your sponsor in a committed and sustained manner that will be there during the times when your project has issues? Will your sponsor be willing to support the effort when the political headwinds are blowing in their face or will they run for cover and just throw you under the bus?

You can be certain that every project will have its moment of crisis. I've had projects that seemed like they were always in a crisis. You should do everything you can to develop and maintain the relationship with your sponsor. Your best approach is to maintain consistent communications. Follow the *CFS Checklist* to mitigate your risks and improve the quality of your communications.

Do your team members see the project the same way or does everyone have a different explanation of what it means? In many ways, it reminds me of the old story when three blind men are asked to describe the elephant that's in the room and each one has a different description of what they are touching.

To obtain the "buy in" when you need to make a significant change, you need to identify your key stakeholders and develop a relationship with them. You want to make sure the stakeholders know the role they will play on the project.

As a first step, you should write down what you need from your sponsors, then have a discussion to make sure you have their agreement for support with their organizations and with their bosses. Too many times, I've seen issues when you don't follow this step because there is a process of socialization and understanding that must be achieved to obtain support.

Once you've had the discussions and obtained support, then develop a communication statement for the stakeholders to send to their organizations. Make it easy for them to support you by communicating with clear and concise updates. Don't wait for them to write something up and send it out. Over service your sponsor and make everything so easy, that they can't say no.

Your next step is to identify shadow stakeholders that exist in the organization. You'll want to identify any individuals in the organization that may have competing interests. When you are leading a transformation project you will have people who are threatened by the change that you are putting in place. They will view the project as having a negative impact to their organization or their own personnel success.

Regardless, you must work with them to educate and identify how they can support the effort. Find a way to link their interests to the success of your project. It will take some work but focus on the key facts that will improve from the investment being made. Stick with it, they will eventually come around.

CHAPTER 7

Agile Project Management (APM) Checklist

[Keeping the Scrum Master on Track]

"THOSE WHO PLAN DO BETTER THAN THOSE WHO
DO NOT PLAN, EVEN THOUGH THEY
RARELY STICK TO THEIR PLAN."

-SIR WINSTON CHURCHILL

Agile is a methodology that was developed in the software industry to address the issues in the traditional waterfall method of development. Agile is a way to continually press forward and make progress with your team in a highly collaborative manner. You'll typically go through three phases in the project.

- Release Planning
- Sprint Planning
- Sprint Execution

The Agile methodology has many variations but most of the same components across development organizations. The scrum board, using Lean techniques, burndown, and achieving velocity are usually common across most teams.

I developed the *APM Checklist* to help you follow the Agile methodology and get the most value from it.

I use it to manage internal teams and vendors when developing software. In many cases, the vendors I've seen will either have a really good internal process or they won't. When you assess their capabilities, the *APM Checklist* is a good tool to evaluate the vendor's processes.

Steps for APM Checklist	Complete Y/N
User Stories developed	
Prioritize using the Kanban Board	
Create a Day in the Life for the future state when the project is complete/implemented	
Map the user stories to the sprints/iterations	
Finalize estimate/milestones	
Develop the test cases based on the user stories to identify the scenarios in testing	
Follow the CFS Checklist for effective communication with the Product Owner and Organization	
Execution	
Daily stand up	
Testing/Validation of features	
Update key metrics for sprint/iteration	
Make adjustments to backlog/priorities	
Release	
Review work completed and validation of changes	
Review with customer/key stakeholders	
Brainstorm changes/adjust plan and milestones	
Deployment	

The *APM Checklist* has a planning section and an execution section. The planning session consists of:

Developing the User Stories - This is the basis of the requirements for the project. It creates the set of requirements that will become the new product, system or enhancement.

Prioritize using the Kanban Board - During this step you go through the first set of prioritizing the feature sets to be developed. This will continue throughout your project as you constantly balance your schedule and progress.

Create a *Day in the Life (DITL)* for the future state - This is an activity that puts together in a one-page summary the future state once the project is complete. In my opinion this brings to life all the user stories so that you can connect the dots for the future state. It's a good tool to use with the customer to validate the whole project rather than individual user stories.

Map the user stories to the sprints/iterations - Your schedule usually dictates the number of sprints that you will use during the development cycle and you "chunk the user stories" into those time slots on the schedule.

Finalize your estimate/milestones - You should be able to put together an estimate for the customer and the schedule after going through the up-front work to define the project.

Develop the test cases based on the user stories and acceptance criteria to identify the scenarios in testing - This is a task that is off the traditional Agile framework, but I've found it helpful to improve the quality of the deliverables. You take the user stories and put together the test cases for how you will test the functionality. This clarifies the key things the developer will need to code into the project so that your defect rate is reduced. I put this step in because many times the details for edits and logic are at a high level in the acceptance criteria and this reduces some of the ambiguity.

Follow the *CFS Checklist* for effective communication with the Product Owner and Organization - This should be followed during the design, execution and for the release. Communication is critical to keeping everyone on the same page and you're typically doing it with the team, but the project sponsor is sometimes left out of the process until the end. In my experience, it's better to keep the sponsor in the loop. Following the *CFS Checklist* will make them a part of the process and build a partnership.

Execution - This is the sprint execution, where you start each day with a standup that is concise, clear and focuses on what needs to be done specifically for that day. An experienced scrum master is keeping the bigger picture in mind but is guiding the team to be focused on the current deliverables. The sprint will be a defined period of time with clear deliverables (completion of user stories), that includes testing, updating the schedule, identifying the escapes (defects) when testing and the constant adjustments to the backlog and priorities.

Release - This is your validation and verification stage prior to the production release for the product. With Agile, it forces the release of a product that constantly improves the product. You will review all the work completed and validate the test results. You will review the escapes that occurred during testing and determine if they will go into the final release based on additional testing. The customer is a partner in this phase and should work with you to help you prioritize and make some of the business decisions that must be made for the release.

Deployment - This wraps up the activities that were completed during the sprint and completes the communications that go along with the deployment of the new capability.

I began my career as a software developer and the development methodology at the time was the traditional waterfall method. The process was very rigid and didn't work well with most projects since it was built on getting the requirement specification agreed upon before you would turn it over to the development team to finish.

There were regular reviews and status updates, but so much of the code would be developed before the user had a chance for it to be tested and therefore, many times it would not meet expectations. In some cases, the user didn't really know what they wanted but only knew that what they had didn't work well. Others wanted to radically change the tool to meet a new demand. We didn't have the tools or processes that are really good in Agile such as the user stories, Kanban boards and the daily standups to have a good feedback loop.

The upfront work required to address a new design, product or feature is still the area that people want to short cut. Whether it was the Waterfall or the Agile method, people are inclined to take a short cut during development. I've worked in the architecture and engineering fields and the same mentality exists regardless if you can see a building's blueprint or if they can't describe a feature that they want in a new product. They still require the effort of engineering hours up front to design a proper solution.

Many projects I've seen have too much of the *Activity Without a Plan (AWP)* mindset. They just start building something and they will let you know if it's right when it's done. You might as well tell a builder to go to the building site and get started without the architectural drawings, the geology report and the material specifications. It's the wrong approach and will get you in trouble every time.

The Agile framework works great if you've done the up-front work and you have a scrum master who knows the methodology and is disciplined in their approach. The scrum master fills the project manager's role in Agile. Sadly, I haven't seen many organizations that demand the discipline with the scrum master. The *APM Checklist* can be used with the scrum master to keep standard work a part of the Agile framework. Frequently, I've seen scrum masters who will follow a subset of the framework or have come up with their own approach that will vary from project to project. I have seen brilliant people who seem to pull things off with their own unique approach, but they are the exception.

Your approach to develop user stories is a collaboration and brainstorming session with your client. You will use storyboarding, brainstorming, prioritizing with affinity diagrams and the Kanban board. This is a critical piece to get right and document the "to be" state so it forces people to actually think through the design and the process.

Even when things appear simple, they aren't and require more work than you think. I like to use an example when people want to "gloss over" the details necessary to perform detailed task level work. I lead a short exercise to flowchart all the steps it takes to change a flat tire. No, you don't get to call AAA in this example. When you go through this exercise, you realize that something you think is simple becomes more involved and more complex than you think it should.

CHAPTER 8

Communicate for Success(CFS) Checklist

[You tell the story best]

"FACTS TELL, STORIES SELL."

— ANONYMOUS

C ommunication is a critical element for managing projects effectively. For projects that are large in scope ($300K+), I would identify a resource that was assigned to develop the communications that are needed to keep a large, complex project on task. A good communications resource is worth their weight in gold because as a project manager, you spend most of your time focused on execution and managing the daily problems. It's the "whack a mole" game that you play every day as a project manager.

Problems and issues always pop up and you must resolve those issues quickly. Managing change is a critical part of successful project management. You manage change through effective communication. A part of every project is changing the current state to something better and being able to communicate that effectively will increase your chances for success. Problems typically leave you with little time to communicate. It reminds me of a Shakespeare play and King Richard III's famous phrase, "a horse, a horse, my kingdom for a horse". The phrase is repeated ironically, when someone needs some insignificant item.

Shakespeare shows that the value and importance of things may change suddenly, and basic resources, like a horse in battle, could become more important than a whole kingdom. Communication is the life blood of your project and you may have that same sense about communications sometimes because it's so critical that it be done well.

How to solve the communication issues and keep your team on track is a critical component for project management. You should have a repeatable process and follow it to stay on track. The *Communicate for Success (CFS) Checklist* will keep you focused and has the following steps:

Steps for CFS Checklist	Complete Y/N
Sponsor communication to the organization	
Stakeholder Meeting to review the DITL	
Weekly Key Message communicated for the project	
Monthly Updates for budget & schedule	
Recurring Meetings	
1 on 1 with your primary sponsor	
Stakeholder meetings to review the key project areas (action items, cost, budget, schedule, technical)	
Team Meetings	
Change review board	
Executive reviews	
Project artifacts	
Weekly Project status	
Scope change log	
Schedule impacts	
Resource Changes	
Post the updates in your collaboration space	

Your sponsor's input is an essential element to make sure the support for your project is sustained.

Work with your sponsor to develop a communication plan that affirms their support and the reasons for putting the project in place. Draft a communication plan that you can use when you meet with your sponsor to develop the formal communications that they will send to their peers and other key executives in the organization. Create a set of talking points for the sponsor, which they will repeat in various meetings and when there are other opportunities to discuss the value of the project.

The next step is to meet with the primary stakeholders to discuss the *DITL* that was developed as the vision for what's different when you're finished. It's the "to be" state that addresses the current state problems and is the reason you're putting the new capabilities in place. Use this session as the opportunity to address any issues that may not have surfaced so you know the areas you need to focus on to achieve a successful outcome.

Not everyone will support the project in the way that you would like, and you will need multiple communication channels to achieve the support and buy-in needed for your project. There will be some people in the organization that may oppose the project for whatever reason, but your best defense is to communicate effectively using the *CFS Checklist*.

The next step is to put together a key message for your project every week. This message will highlight the activities for the project. It could be as simple as the following:

> "This week the project completed the release of a working prototype that is being used to test our concept and the finance organization has provided positive feedback during testing. Our project has completed 15 of the 45 critical milestones and spent $73,800 of the $204,000 budget. We're on schedule and under budget as of today. Budget is underrunning as a result of finding some productivity improvements

during the testing process which meant less labor was allocated. We'd like to recognize Ali Jones, who was instrumental in setting up the test environment to complete our deliverables on time this week."

This message should go to the sponsor, key stakeholders and your project team members. This weekly communication keeps everyone informed on your progress and is one of the methods for keeping your project sold. You're not only a project manager, but a marketing and branding resource for the project. By following the *CFS Checklist* you will keep your critical stakeholders informed of progress that allows them to better support your efforts.

Every month you will update your project schedule for milestones and your budget status. Depending upon the complexity of the project, you can use a one-page summary Gantt chart like the example below as well:

Salesforce Service Cloud rollout

Task		Owner	S	W1 Aug 5	W2 Aug 12	W3 Aug 19	W4 Aug 26	W5 Sep 2	W6 Sep 9	W7 Sep 16	W8 Sep 23	W9 Sep 30	W10 Oct 7	W11 Oct 14	W12 Oct 21	Cost
1	Develop scope, charter and draft plan for Service Cloud			████												$1,800 / $1,800
2	Hold process mapping event with the Call Center				██											$10,000 / $10,000
3	Develop requirements for Implementation partner					████										$5,000 / $5,000
4	Select Implementation partner and complete project planning						███									$2,000 / $2,000
5	Evaluate and determine the data quality and migration plans							███								$4,000 / $4,000
6	Develop the to be state and process mapping from "as-is"								███							$8,000 / $8,000
7	Evaluate unique customer id and interface impacts								██████							$3,000 / $3,000
8	Select CTI app and integrate with Salesforce									███						$15,000 / $15,000
9	Identify additional 3rd party apps for Service Cloud								██████							$5,000 / $5,000
10	Training and use cases									███						$6,000 / $6,000
11	Service Cloud implementation											███				$10,000 / $10,000
12	Go Live												███		$4,000 / $4,000

Definition of Success		S	Current Status		Cost Summary
1	Interface functions flawlessly in performance and mapping of data between all systems	1			$73,800
2		2			$73,800
3		3			$0

Page 1 of 1

For a budget status, I use a simple format that tracks expenses and capital.

Service Cloud Rollout					
*week ending 06/09/15					
	Act		Bgt		Bal
Internal	$	25,476	$	77,000	$	51,524
Capital	$	12,100	$	32,000	$	19,900
Expense	$	13,376	$	45,000	$	31,624
Outsourced development	$	15,314	$	58,000	$	42,686
Capital	$	5,000	$	30,000	$	25,000
Expense	$	10,314	$	28,000	$	17,686
Marketing	$	32,433	$	40,000	$	7,567
Capital	$	-	$	-	$	-
Expense	$	32,433	$	40,000	$	7,567
Other Capital	$	-	$	28,600	$	28,600
Total Capital	$	17,100	$	90,600	$	73,500
Total Expense	$	56,123	$	113,000	$	56,877
Total Spend	$	73,223	$	203,600	$	130,377
		36%				64%
FES Lab. not Cap.	$	47,541				
*Internal Labor Expense is illustrated here to show total impact, but is not counted in our budget balance calculation.					

Recurring meetings should be set up with your sponsor on a monthly basis to maintain effective communications and obtain feedback on the project. This is a session to work any issues, solicit advise and share feedback from your sponsor. In these sessions, work on your talking points until you have something that is clear and concise. Then, you and the sponsor are on the same page to advance the support of the project.

The stakeholder meetings should be scheduled monthly or more frequently, depending upon where you are in the lifecycle of your project. Typically, you might need more frequent sessions during the startup, or if you're not meeting your targets. In these sessions you want to have an agenda that covers the following areas:

Action item log – Maintain a current list of open actions with their current status.

Milestone status – You can use the example provided in Chapter 5 as an example or something that provides a clear picture of your project.

Scope management - Address any areas that are unclear and if you're seeing any creep in the requirements.

Risk Register – Maintain a list of risks, their impact if realized and mitigations for the risks.

Communication – Provide feedback on the areas in the *CFS Checklist*.

Cost performance – Provide an update on your current spend to the budget and if you're seeing any issues.

Overall project performance – Provide feedback on the overall project. I use a Green/Yellow/Red color coding on each category that was used in the example in Chapter 5. This is an example of a project dashboard that can be used:

Category	Status	Comments
Resource Status	Y	Production issues impacting project
Milestone Status	R	Milestone slips reflect resource issues
Scope Management	G	Scope definition completed before project initiation and change board in place for managing any changes
Communication	G	All Stakeholders briefed with regular updates
Cost Status	Y	Holding end date based on new resource commitments
Overall Program	Y	Team must remain focused to meet the end date

Your team meetings should be weekly once you've established the foundation for your project. During the startup phase it might be more frequent as you're completing the definition and assignment of resources. It takes a few weeks to build your business rhythms and for everyone to become comfortable with the process. This is part of the change management process that you are putting in place. Communication is a critical piece of effective change management.

It's even more important today with all the interruptions that people are bombarded with inside and outside of the workplace. Being present and in the moment seems to be a constant challenge for everyone.

Put a change management review board in place if your project is large, complex and spans four months or more. The review board should consist of the key stakeholders that you've identified and key technical personnel who are supporting the project and your customer representative. Changes that impact cost and schedule should be reviewed in the meeting for approval. Every project seems to deviate from the original plan and scope, so you want to be laser focused on managing the change.

Some changes are needed if they are business critical and some are not if they are solving a problem for a person or organization that was not a part of the original scope. I've had many customers that want to keep changing direction because they aren't aware of the cost impact. When a change is requested, you should provide the cost impact for the added scope and its cost impact to the schedule. The customer will need to approve those changes before you take any action that impacts your current budget or schedule.

Executive reviews are put in place to provide awareness, socialize the new concept, work the "buy-in" with the senior team and to obtain support for the change within their organizations. These meetings should be monthly or quarterly depending upon how much support is required and should focus on the key elements that are as follows:

- Tell them up front why they are here and what you need from them.
- Recap what happened in the prior meeting and review the agenda for the current meeting.
- Always have an updated schedule as they will want to know when it will be completed.
- Know your budget and have the summary updated that was reviewed earlier in the chapter.
- Provide any talking points you want them to have that can help them better describe the project.

- Provide an agenda and keep the meeting on point.
- Always provide a follow-up summary and identify any action items that were given in the meeting.
- Post all updates in your collaboration space to ensure everyone has a single "version of the truth".

Remember, you are the brand manager, the storyteller and the accountable resource for making this project successful. The bottom line is to communicate, communicate again and keep communicating throughout the project.

CHAPTER 9

Metrics

*[Sometimes you have to torture
the data to get the answer]*

"WHAT'S MEASURED IMPROVES"

-PETER DRUCKER

Early in my career, I didn't understand from a practitioner perspective, the required metrics and mechanisms necessary to deliver successful projects. When I worked for General Electric, I had the good fortune to rotate outside my role in Information Technology and take a functional job running the quality organization and later running manufacturing operations. The lessons I learned in that short time have stuck with me throughout my career.

It was my first day as the quality manager, and after the "all hands" meeting announcing the new organization and my new position, I headed back to my office to get started. I found a government issued document called a *Quality Deficiency Report (QDR)* on my desk. I didn't even know what a *QDR* was, much less what it meant. But of course, my boss dropped by since he was told about it and he explained to me that it was very bad, and they came in varying levels of severity. I was given a "Method A" which was equivalent to a warning. A more extreme action would be a "Method C", which meant you were not able to issue purchase orders without government approval.

This was many years ago and the government has now evolved with identification of deficiencies and has changed the reporting characteristics. However, it's still a tool to document issues that can have significant impact on your job and company. My boss explained that I was here to fix the problem and if we got a "Method C", I would be fired immediately.

When working in a manufacturing environment, you must have an intense focus on identifying and resolving problems in real time. Production moves quickly and you need to be proactive in your approach.

Needless to say, I was motivated to understand quality as an organization and identify the necessary metrics to make sure I wasn't fired due to an unforeseen *QDR*. Relationships matter, which I speak about throughout the book. It is just as important to make make sure you don't have surprises on the work you manage. ***No*** *one likes surprises*. Using metrics effectively and managing your relationships are two risk mitigations that everyone should pay close attention to as they manage projects.

On another occasion I was called into a project manager's office who was responsible for a flight simulation training product that we built. Some of these simulators contained 5,000+ printed circuit boards to provide the processing power to support the simulations. The project manager showed me a board that had bent pins going into the sockets for all the Integrated Circuits (IC's). As a productivity measure, manufacturing had obtained an automated insertion machine. Unfortunately, the machine wasn't calibrated properly when the IC's were inserted into their sockets on the circuit boards.

The circuit boards passed the continuity test, but the physical inspection missed the bent pins. The project manager proceeded to ream me out about our quality and wanted to know what the hell was I going to do about it. The project manager had 30 years of experience and I had 8. This was my first assignment in the quality organization, and I wanted to do it well.

I had always been very close to the manufacturing operations in a number of roles but had never been directly responsible for product quality. Needless to say, I was somewhat intimidated and embarrassed by the results of an organization where I was responsible for the quality of the product. I committed to address the issue and get back to him with a plan. He had little patience for my lack of experience and wanted a plan by the following morning.

He said on departing, "I don't want any high-level overviews, I want a specific plan that addresses this issue".

What an embarrassment for the company and for me. When you present something to a customer and it's clear there's a quality issue you must be responsive, competent and comprehensive in your response. I can't blame the project manager for "reaming" me on the issue. I was, after all, the quality manager and I'm sure the customer had done the same to him. Remember, no one likes a surprise, especially when it comes at the end of the project. These simulators cost millions of dollars depending upon the configuration and needs. They were all custom built to the client's requirements and extremely expensive.

I had the crap scared out of me when I went to the factory floor and did several inspections on current work in process and found that the issue was indeed being repeated. I shut down the line and called a meeting with the operators, inspectors and maintenance teams to discuss the issue and get their thoughts on the corrective action.

After reviewing the procedures and practices for maintaining the machine, we found that we missed some critical calibration times which were necessary to ensure the machine was operating properly.

We had a project in place where we were working with our local government quality team on a total quality initiative and were starting to implement *Statistical Process Control (SPC)* metrics in several areas. This seemed like a perfect application.

I had several quality engineers on the floor, and they put a process in place at the IC insertion machine to record the results after each board was completed. We started identifying the root cause of the problem. The "bent legs" problem was solved by becoming data driven in our processes and it's a lesson I've carried forward throughout my career.

Many of the projects I manage today are Information Technology projects, but the parallels to manufacturing are very similar.

Throughout my career, I've found that there are three metrics, applicable across any organization discipline which really drive continuous improvement.

Those metrics are:

QUALITY, UNIT COSTS AND TOTAL CYCLE TIME

QUALITY

Quality is the primary metric to determine if you're meeting expectations or failing to do so. Quality can be represented by the product quality that's being provided and represents the variation in the product or service. Low variation is a sign of quality because it's repeatable. High variation is indicative of poor quality since it's not being repeated in a consistent manner. Delivering an invoice has a quality measurement (is it accurate, timely, descriptive) as well as correcting a software issue on your laptop (timely, responsive, and effective communication).

Quality is always free and smart business managers understand this point. W. Edward Deming is credited with the Total Quality movement that transformed the Japanese economy in the 1960's through a focus on continuous improvement. Quality has a direct reflection on customer satisfaction. Quality determines repeat business, affects your brand and builds your image.

UNIT COSTS

Unit costs provides another critical element that should be used to drive continuous improvement. Identify if the issues are cost or volume related and how much waste is built into your processes. Unit costs are key whether you are in engineering, finance, information technology, manufacturing, or sales.

Unit costs provide key visibility into your efficiency and effectiveness like no other metric. I know a company that sold their product for $29.99 and because they knew that a return would cost them $150 to document, process and resend to the customer, they told the customer to keep it and they would send a replacement. Some companies don't understand their return costs and lose more money on each return due to their inefficiencies in the process.

It also helps address the issue where volume increases impact your total costs. If unit costs are decreasing, then you're taking the right actions.

TOTAL CYCLE TIME

Total cycle time is the third metric that provides critical insight into your efficiencies impacting both customer and employee satisfaction. The cycle time metric applies to every functional discipline and should be measured as a part of continuous improvement. The cycle time metric should be in place for every internal business process, whether it's for creating an engineering drawing, processing an invoice or collecting cash.

You should have a baseline in place and constantly identify improvements in your process to reduce your total cycle time by eliminating waste and reducing your costs.

There are many metrics that can be used, but these metrics will drive real change in the way you manage your projects and deliver results. They should be a part of any project manager's toolkit to use as you develop your *DITL* vision or when you're putting together the business case to transform your business.

In the next chapter, we're going to discuss the critical metrics that are used to manage your cost and schedule. The *MYS Checklist* will be your guide to managing your projects successfully.

CHAPTER 10

Manage Your Schedule (MYS) Checklist

[Critical metrics for cost and schedule]

"BETTER THREE HOURS TOO SOON,
THAN ONE MINUTE TOO LATE"

- WILLIAM SHAKESPEARE

M anaging your schedule is a primary focus of any project manager. We live and die by how we perform on our schedule. The *MYS Checklist* is about change management. It involves the technical management and the communication that provides a picture of how the schedule is progressing or whether it's missing key milestones.

As the project manager, you are monitoring your critical milestones, coordinating with your resources and making sure you have no surprises. In today's environment you have people in different locations, little face to face communications and a lot of digital distractions that constantly interrupt your day to day routine. Being able to focus without interruptions is a challenge when you face the avalanche of electronic pests that attack you each day. This reminds me of the Nutrisystem commercial where they tell you "if you want to lose the weight, put down the pie". Just put down the phone and be present where your feet are located!

Nothing is more important than being able to deliver your project on schedule and on budget. These are the two most important deliverables for managing any project. You can make a lot of mistakes as a project manager but delivering on time and on budget will mitigate many of those mistakes. I'm not advocating forgetting about everything else but do focus on meeting your budget and schedule.

The *MYS Checklist* will give you a simple tool and approach to keep you and your team focused to meet your schedule commitments. Implement and then repeat the steps each week and the quality of your work will improve.

Steps for MYS Checklist	Complete Y/N
Update Schedule weekly for activity	
Weekly project meeting	
Key Metrics	
Update Percent complete for each critical milestone	
Update Cost Performance index	
Update Schedule Performance Index	
Resources	
Update shared resource spreadsheet for tracking progress	
Review vacation schedule and any resource conflicts	
Review risk register and identify any changes	
Review schedule against the scope of the project and identify if there is out of scope work being performed	
Post the updates in your collaboration space	

In the *MYS Checklist*, you have a clear set of steps to follow to achieve your goals for meeting the schedule. Each week you should do the following:

- Update your schedule to reflect new activities and accomplishments. This is typically your Gantt chart or high-level summary that you use to communicate across your stakeholders.
- Use the following metrics to keep you on the right path. *Earned Value Management (EVM)* is part of the calculation for both the *Cost Performance Index (CPI)* and *Schedule Performance Index (SPI)* metrics. *CPI* and *SPI* are critical

metrics that provide early insight into how you're performing on two of the most critical metrics of any project.

EVM helps project managers measure project performance. It is a systematic project management process used to find variances in projects based on the comparison of worked performed and work planned. *EVM* is used on cost and schedule control and is useful for predicting future performance. Many of your project management tools can calculate *EVM* for you, but if you want to understand the mechanics, please review the following:

EVM IS CALCULATED AS FOLLOWS:

- *Planned Value (PV)* — The budgeted cost of the work scheduled to be completed on an activity or *WBS* component up to a given point in time
- *Actual Cost (AC)* — The total expenditure for the work on the schedule activity or *WBS* component during a given time period
- *Earned Value (EV)* — The budgeted value for the work completed on the schedule activity or *WBS* component during a given time period

COST PERFORMANCE INDEX (CPI)

The *Cost Performance Index (CPI)* helps you analyze the efficiency of the cost utilized by the project. It measures the value of the work completed compared to the actual cost spent on the project.

According to the *PMBOK* Guide "The *Cost Performance Index (CPI)* is a measure of the cost efficiency of budgeted resources, expressed as a ratio of earned value to actual cost".

In simple terms, the *Cost Performance Index (CPI)* informs you of how much you are earning for each dollar spent on the project. The *Cost Performance Index (CPI)* is an indication of the cost performance of the project.

Cost Performance Index (*CPI)* = (Earned Value) / (Actual Cost)

$$CPI = EV / AC$$

WITH THE REFERENCED FORMULA YOU CAN CONCLUDE:

- If the *CPI* is less than one, you are earning less than you are spending. You are over budget.
- If the *CPI* is greater than one, you are earning more than you are spending. You are under budget.
- If the *CPI* is equal to one, this means earning and spending are equal. You can say that you are proceeding exactly per the planned budget spending, although this rarely happens.

EXAMPLE USING THE *COST PERFORMANCE INDEX (CPI)*

You have a project that will be completed in 12 months and the cost of the project is $100,000 USD. Six months have passed, and $60,000 USD has been spent, but on closer review you find that only 40% of the work has been completed so far.

Find the *CPI* for this project and deduce whether you are under budget or over budget.

GIVEN VALUES:

- *Actual Cost (AC)* = $60,000 USD
- *Planned Value (PV)* = 50% of $100,000 USD = $50,000 USD
- *Earned Value (EV)* = 40% of $100,000 USD = $40,000 USD
- *Cost Performance Index (CPI)* = *EV / AC*
- *CPI* = $40,000 / $60,000 = 0.67

Since the *CPI* is less than one, this means you are earning $0.67 USD for every $1 USD spent. In other words, you are over budget.

A consistently high or low value of *SPI* or *CPI* is an indication that something is wrong with your planning and/or the cost estimates. In this case, check all assumptions and estimates for their correctness and take corrective action as needed.

SCHEDULE PERFORMANCE INDEX (SPI)

According to the *PMBOK* Guide, "The *Schedule Performance Index (SPI)* is a measure of schedule efficiency expressed as the ratio of earned value to planned value".

The Schedule Performance Index (SPI) provides information about the schedule performance of the project. It is the efficiency of the time utilized on the project.

The *Schedule Performance Index (SPI)* can be determined by dividing earned value by planned value.

Schedule Performance Index (SPI) = (Earned Value) / (Planned Value)

$SPI = EV / PV$

WITH THE REFERENCED FORMULA YOU CAN CONCLUDE:

- If the *SPI* is greater than one, this means more work has been completed than the planned work. You are ahead of schedule.
- If the *SPI* is less than one, this means less work has been completed than the planned work. You are behind schedule.
- If the *SPI* is equal to one, the completed work is equal to the planned work. Your project is on schedule.

EXAMPLES USING SPI CALCULATIONS:

You have a project to be completed in 12 months and the cost of the project is $100,000 USD. Six months have passed, and $60,000 USD has been spent, but on closer review you find that only 40% of the work has been completed so far.

GIVEN IN THE QUESTION:

- *Actual Cost (AC)* = $60,000 USD
- *Planned Value (PV)* = 50% of $100,000 USD = $50,000 USD
- *Earned Value (EV)* = 40% of $100,000 USD = $40,000 USD
- *Schedule Performance Index (SPI)* = *EV / PV*
- *SPI* = $40,000 / $50,000 = 0.8

Since the *SPI* is less than one, you are behind schedule.

EARNED VALUE MANAGEMENT (EVM) IS THE KEY TO MANAGING YOUR PROJECT SUCCESSFULLY AND DELIVERING ON TIME AND ON BUDGET.

The following metrics should be used to help you deliver consistently:

- *Baseline* - Snapshot of the project plan when contract is awarded, or the project is authorized

- *Percent Complete* - Estimated percent of the work that has been completed
- *Actual Cost (AC)* - The total expenditure for the work on the schedule activity or *WBS* component during a given time period
- *Estimate to Complete (ETC)* – Estimated costs required to finish each phase
- *Estimate at Completion (EAC)* - The *EAC* is compared to the baseline. $EAC = AC + ETC$
- *Planned Value (PV)* - The budgeted cost of the work scheduled to be completed on an activity or *WBS* component up to a given point in time
- *Earned Value (EV)* - The budgeted value for the work completed on the schedule activity or *WBS* component during a given time period
- *Cost Performance Index (CPI) = EV/AC*
- *Schedule Performance Index (SPI) = EV/ PV*
- *Schedule Variance (SV) = EV-PV*

Let's use an example and work through it so you have a clear understanding of how to use the data.

We start with a project that has the total costs estimated at $100,000 over a six-month period.

The costs are time phased and are estimated as follows:

- 1st month - $10,000
- 2nd month - $20,000

- 3rd month - $20,000
- 4th month - $25,000
- 5th month - $15,000
- 6th month - $10,000

We just completed month 3 and our actual costs are $40,000. Our earned value based on the work we've actually completed per the *WBS* is $30,000. We had a team meeting to review the cost and schedule assumptions with the key stakeholders. Based on the inputs and the review of the *WBS*, the team provided a new *ETC* for the project of $70,000.

The calculations for *CPI* and *SPI* would be:

- *Planned Value (PV)* = $50K
- *Actual Cost (CV)* = $40K
- *Estimate to Complete (ETC)* = $70K
- *Earned Value (EV)* = $30K
- *Estimate at Completion (EAC)* = *AC + ETC*
    $110K = $40K + $70K
- *Cost Performance Index (CPI)* = *EV/AC*
    CPI = $30K/$40K = .75 (Negative since < 1)
- *Schedule Performance Index (SPI)* = *EV/ PV*
    SPI = $30K/$50K = .6 (Negative since < 1)
- *Schedule Variance (SV)* = *EV-PV*
    SV = 30K-$50K = $20K (Negative since < 0)

The project is behind schedule and has a significant schedule variance. We're halfway through the project timeline and our key indicators show that we are in trouble. This could mean you haven't brought on the resources you planned to accomplish the work needed or some assumptions may have changed. As a result, you will need to examine your tasks and schedule if you want to meet your targets. The reasons may be many, but you've identified the issues early and hopefully you can address them without impacting the cost or the schedule.

Earned value is a single data point and there may be other issues that occurred that aren't detrimental to your project. You could have ordered equipment earlier than planned to mitigate some risks that will be positive for the project.

Use *EVM* as an early warning system because no one likes to have a surprise during the last phase of the project. It's the common occurrence of you are on plan until you're not and you have a surprise which no one likes. Costs rarely occur as they are planned, so recognize the data point and use it wisely as one of the tools in your portfolio.

COMMUNICATION

Communicating weekly is critical to managing the change in the environment. Use the *CFS Checklist* as discussed in Chapter 8. It covers everything you'll need to be effective in your communication.

The key elements are:

- Update your schedule for the most recent activity. This information will become the weekly message for the project team that you want them to know on a regular basis
- This includes any relevant events that the team should have on their calendar (meetings, vendor updates, team meetings, current schedule, progress, risks)
- The project meeting/call is used to quickly communicate relevant information and clarify any questions that are identified from the team
- Update your key metrics (% complete, *CPI, SPI, EVM,* etc.)
- Review vacation schedules, any conflicts with your team resources and identify mitigations if needed
- Review the risk register in the weekly team meeting to make sure you remain current on any risks for your project
- Review schedule against the scope and identify if you have any scope changes

Collecting and staying focused on the data is critical for successful project management. I like to reference the saying that I'm sure you've all heard, "What gets measured gets done". Focus on your metrics and communications.

CHAPTER 11

Closing Projects Successfully (CPS) Checklist

[It's time to take your Victory Lap]

"FIRST, HAVE A DEFINITE, CLEAR PRACTICAL IDEAL;
A GOAL, AN OBJECTIVE. SECOND, HAVE THE
NECESSARY MEANS TO ACHIEVE YOUR ENDS;
WISDOM, MONEY, MATERIALS, AND METHODS. THIRD,
ADJUST ALL YOUR MEANS TO THAT END."

- ARISTOTLE

You've followed the *Five Simple Checklists* approach and the results of the project have been successfully delivered to your customer. Well done! Your team did an outstanding job and now some of the team members have other opportunities for increased responsibilities due to the valuable skills they demonstrated in a challenging environment.

The CPS Checklist will provide you with the steps to close out your project and develop a continuous improvement approach across your organization for managing projects.

Steps for CPS Checklist	Complete Y/N
Review original scope and final scope for deltas	
Develop final scope statement with a summary of how it met or didn't meet the original targets	
Lessons Learned	
Team meeting to brainstorm the lessons learned during the project	
Document the Lessons Learned	
Customer	
Review the final scope and accomplishments	
Review Lessons Learned during the project	
Identify changes to put in place to improve our processes	
Review all charges and shut down the project budget	
Identify the ongoing requirements needed to sustain the efforts if needed	
Document the key points and send to key stakeholders	
Celebrate	

Typically, what you were tasked to do in the beginning changed and you managed the change process using your *CFS Checklist*.

As you look at the original scope and identify the deltas you will develop a final scope statement for the team and your customer. This will provide an opportunity for you to examine areas that didn't work as well as those that did. As a project manager, you must be a problem solver who finds a way to achieve results in spite of unexpected setbacks. You've made it through this book, so you must be motivated to function and achieve at a high level.

The next step is to document the final scope that reflects what you actually did and how it compares to your original scope. This is a good exercise to go through, so you can learn how to better develop your scope statement the next time. Maybe you didn't have all the key stakeholders included and as you got into the project unknown requirements surfaced that you had to address.

Next, you will need to conduct a final, short team meeting to brainstorm the "Lessons Learned" so the organization can continue to improve. I find this works better with food. ☺ Good food is preferable.

Hand everyone a post-it note stack and have them start writing one item per post-it note at a time. Place those on a board and group them based on what was written down. This is a really short exercise and once you've accumulated the items in similar groups, discuss as a team, eliminate duplicates and you have your lessons learned.

Now it is time to close out with your customer using the artifacts you've developed. You'll have your final scope statement and the deltas to the original as well as some commentary on the major points. You have the lessons learned from your team meeting that you've incorporated into a form that will be clear and concise. If you've identified changes that should be made with procedures or processes, you'll have those identified as well.

Hopefully, your project was wildly successful, and the customer is receptive to all that you and your team have accomplished, but what happens if the project is considered a failure? It happens more than most people like to acknowledge, but you should still go through this process. At the end of the day, it's about continuous improvement and learning in your organization. Providing the scope deltas and the lessons learned will help you get better.

The financial matters, and any associated charge numbers, need to be taken care of to close out the project. You need to plan for next year if this project requires ongoing resources to continue to operate and support the company. I've seen too many times when a project manager neglects this task and it causes a lot of pain since it's not reflected in next year's budget after people have come to depend on it to do their jobs.

After you've completed the review with the customer, closed your financial responsibilities, then you can put together a summary for the stakeholders that supported you through the process. Let your stakeholders know how their support impacted the results.

And lastly, celebrate with the participants. The size and scope of the celebration will vary, but at a minimum have lunch, a dinner or a cake where results can be celebrated. Take pictures and put several in your company newsletter so that the entire company will be aware of the actions and results. Take time to thank everyone for their support. Invite your customer, sponsors, stakeholders and team members to attend and celebrate the accomplishments.

Then, take a deep breath and a sigh of relief, because the next big project is right around the corner! Good luck!

CHAPTER 12

Private Equity

[Operating in real time]

"PEOPLE USED TO THINK THAT PRIVATE EQUITY
WAS BASICALLY JUST A COMPENSATION SCHEME, BUT
IT IS MUCH MORE ABOUT MAKING
COMPANIES MORE EFFICIENT."

-DAVID RUBENSTEIN

I love consulting for *Private Equity Groups (PEGs)* and their portfolio companies. I feel like I have a pulse on the economy by being exposed to so many companies in so many industries (consumer products, federal, health care, oil and gas, professional services, and general services).

The common link in most companies is the single threading of resources and manual processes. There are companies that still use paper timecards that are filled out by the employee and faxed to data entry, then key punched into payroll. The same processes used in the 80's are still alive and well in some of the companies of today. I wish I were kidding, but I've worked with companies that had annual revenues of $700M+ that were still capturing their time manually.

Today, those problems can be solved very easily by off the shelf solutions that work very well, but management will resist making the change. They would rather live with the pain of the existing solution than use technology to solve simple, manual problems. Some companies would embrace the change, but others would resist it. Those that leveraged technology, would tend to do much better when they were sold.

I've worked with many Private Equity portfolio companies and have only run across a few unicorns that were tremendous investments and hit a home run for the *PEGs*. The most successful company I've seen is YETI Coolers, based in Austin Texas. Bought by the Cortec Group in 2012, it was a diamond in the rough that exploded in sales due to organic demand. YETI was founded by two brothers, Roy and Ryan Seiders, who turned the common cooler into a luxury item that people were willing to pay 10X the price of an Igloo to own one.

Roy is the "Steve Jobs" of coolers. He has a passion for the design and was uncompromising in his approach to develop the best product in the market. After Cortec bought the company, the partners for Cortec, David Schnadig and Gene Nesbeda, realized they had a company that could scale and would need the right infrastructure, business systems and personnel to support it. For almost three years, I supported YETI in their transition to invest in technology, build an IT organization and to increase their technical capabilities.

It was so much fun to work with these folks because they were great people and excited about what they were doing. There are very few portfolio companies that have gotten enough scale and can make the investments that YETI Coolers was able to accomplish, eventually leading to a wildly successful IPO.

Private Equity finds opportunities in these companies that are usually founder led or family owned. *PEGs* invest money in the companies to address some of the key risks and acquire companies that create the scale needed to generate a reasonable return in five to eight years depending upon the *PEG*. The first twelve to eighteen months are about investing to address the inefficiencies and improve the processes (eliminate waste, drive a standard work approach and develop a technology roadmap).

The next two years are focused on the acquisitions and scaling the business. Some attention is given to investments, but it's slowing down with most investments and scaling is the highest priority. Year four tends to focus on getting the financials in good shape with a continued focus on increasing revenue and EBITA. In year five or later there is usually little investment and they are preparing to exit the business.

Year five is the beauty pageant for these firms and if they haven't invested in good financial analytics, a CRM and ERP solution, the principles will be crushed with the number of requests that they get during due diligence and the timeline to answer the questions while still doing their day job. The investment banker that's brokering the deal will create a data room that will need to get filled with all manner of requests that potential buyers will want to have answered so they can evaluate the business.

The opportunities are quite dramatic given what can be done from a technology perspective today and the abundance of automation that is available in the marketplace. Most *PEGs* I've worked with are still slow to embrace this since they don't fully understand the value proposition to decrease the operating costs and leverage new technologies. My good friend, Gene Nesbeda at the Cortec Group, always understood the value and how to get it right.

I worked for a portfolio company president that ran a project management company. He didn't see any value in project management and wanted to continue to do business on the back of an envelope. I've had another client think that it was acceptable to have their primary business system four to five releases behind the current version because it was good enough. I've seen over and over the waste and inefficiencies associated with collecting time to bill and the generation of invoices that impact the Order to Cash cycle.

It's not unusual to see companies that may need fifteen days or more to generate weekly invoices. It's not uncommon to see a twenty-five day monthly close cycle.

Some of these issues are because the company didn't recognize the issue and it had always been done that way. Some of it was because the leadership didn't understand the value that could be provided by technology. Almost every PE partner, I've met has been burned on a technology project and that forever makes them skeptical. That's ok.

As a consultant to *PEGs,* my job is to explain the business value and not just the technology. In some companies, you'll run across a leader that is so entrenched in the ways of their past success and are unable to grasp an alternate approach. In many cases, what brought you to the dance will not always get you home. Be nimble, be quick but never be satisfied.

I worked with the President of Franklin Energy, Kevin McDonough who I consider a very good friend. Of course, it didn't start out friendly, since I was the consultant sent in by the Cortec Group to help him and that's not always viewed in a positive manner.

Franklin Energy was very similar to a lot of *PEG* portfolio companies in their approach to running the business. They had a field service organization that was using paper forms to collect information, filling them out while on site, sending them into keypunch and then two weeks later the client would get the report. Of course, you had the quality issues with keypunching a form and the illegibility of handwriting which would cause errors in the final report.

They had to build out a digital solution that would transform their approach and deliver a much better customer experience. We started with a strategy session and built the approach with a timeline to achieve the goals outlined. It took a couple of years, but they completed the implementation and as a result were able to provide a nice return when they were sold in 2016 to Kohlberg & Company. In 2019, Kohlberg sold Franklin Energy to Arbry Partners.

Kevin and I have laughed a lot about his resistance and pushback. But in the end, he took the leap of faith that technology would transform the business and we built out a digital strategy that provided a competitive advantage in the marketplace. At the end, Kevin told me, "To a practitioner, it is obvious but successfully launching a technology is easier said than done. Of course, I never liked paying your bills, but I recognize good advice when I see it and appreciate all the paid and unpaid time you put into making the project a success".

The Cortec Group, particularly Scott Schafler, was pushing for these changes at Franklin Energy and was very supportive during the transformation. Scott is a very wise man, who has seen so much in his lifetime and for whom I have tremendous respect. He is able to keep focused on the prize and move forward, despite dealing with many of the idiosyncrasies common among founder led companies.

Making change is hard anytime you have competing interests. If you look at the business you're in and you look at the critical issues which are holding you back, you'll find these issues will typically be the speed or velocity at which you can make change. Your focus should be to reduce complexity. Technology is a tremendous enabler to improve your business processes and reduce the cost of your operations, but you must focus on a Lean approach with those processes before you introduce any technologies. Adding technology without first addressing the process is a recipe for disaster. You'll end up with more complexity and increased costs.

There are many businesses today that still process information manually, capture information on paper forms and fax it to the home office where it can be key punched into a google doc, a spreadsheet or financial system. These businesses can really knock it out of the park if they leverage the technology available today to simplify their environments.

Utilize the *Five Simple Checklists* as your roadmap for project management.

You can download the templates for the checklists at www.fivesimplechecklists.com by subscribing to our website. I will send you a link to the page that has the templates for you to download after you complete the form.

This approach does not replace the knowledge in the *PMBOK*, it is my consolidated effort on how to apply that knowledge. Understanding project management by studying the *PMBOK* and then testing to obtain certifications in various subject matter areas is important. The *Five Simple Checklists* are tools that can be used to deliver outstanding results without having to be an expert in every knowledge area of the *PMBOK*. Without a doubt, having the *Five Simple Checklists* to guide you is the roadmap for your success.

Let me hear about your project management successes and failures at darthv@fivesimpleChecklists.com.

Index

About The Author

Stephen Hightower is an Information Technology and Management consultant who has been managing projects for over 30 years. He is a Project Management Professional (PMP) and has had extensive program management training with General Electric and Lockheed Martin. During his career he managed projects that saved millions of dollars consolidating IT infrastructure services, delivered multi-million-dollar technology projects to provide new services, including construction and information security projects. In addition, he developed and set up a Program Management Office (PMO) that was used to deliver over $30,000,000 in new infrastructure services for Lockheed Martin annually. He is certified in Information Systems Security and the Lean Six Sigma (LSS) discipline. He has developed training programs for Information Technology teams to deliver services using LSS in addition to managing projects using his *Five Simple Checklists* approach.

Prior to starting his consulting practice, he was the Chief Information Officer for the Global Training and Logistics business unit within Lockheed Martin. He has delivered consulting services across Private Equity and Fortune 500 companies. A sample of these include Barcodes Inc., Cameron Oil and Gas Services, Franklin Energy, Hewlett Packard, Lockheed Martin, NRG Energy, Weiman Products, and YETI Coolers. In his consulting practice, he provides thought leadership with a focus on innovative problem solving while leveraging leading edge technologies. He has extensive relationships with technology vendors and continually evaluates new technologies. He performs due diligence for mergers & acquisitions, business startups, financial turnarounds, corporate reorganizations, and business closures.

Stephen identifies and provides industry best practices for process improvements and efficiencies by developing comprehensive business strategies and improving performance across a number of industry verticals including consumer products, energy conservation, ecommerce, federal, health care, oil and gas, and professional services. His innovative thinking and common sense approach is used to enhance business operations while providing solutions that result in world class service delivery. He develops business strategies that scale and reduce "friction" for the client.

Stephen provides training on using the *Five Simple Checklists* as well as consulting services. You can find additional information for his book by visiting https://fivesimplechecklists.com/

www.ingramcontent.com/pod-product-compliance
Lightning Source LLC
Chambersburg PA
CBHW070340220526
45467CB00001B/193